기초영어 1000문장 말하기 연습 2

박미진 지음

이제 지겨운 '공부'는 그만하고,
'연습'으로 말문을 틔우자!

기초영어
1000문장
말하기연습

토마토
출판사

Speaking Practice - 한국어를 영어로 전환하는 영작 연습

1. 한 페이지에 10문항씩 있어요. 한 문항을 보고 이해하는데 3초, 생각하고 말하는데 3초, 그래서 한 문항당 6초를 소비한다면, 한 페이지에 1분, 100문항을 10분 안에 만드는 연습을 할 수 있어요.

2. 강의를 들으면서 함께해요. 집중하는데 도움도 되고 이해하기도 더 쉬울 거예요.

3. 이제 혼자 말하면서 연습을 해보아요! 녹음기를 켜고 하면 나의 발음도 체크하고, 시간도 체크할 수 있으니 일석이조 이겠죠?

4. 이제 책의 맨 뒷장을 펴고 정답을 확인해 보아요. 강의 들으며 입으로 만들어 보면서 한 번, 글로 보면서 다시 말하면서 두 번, 답 맞추면서 세 번, 이렇게 한 문항을 세 번이나 반복할 수 있어요!

5. 시간이 있다면 마지막엔 글로도 써보세요! 만약 쓰기가 힘들다면 강의를 다시 들으면서 꾸준히 반복적으로 훈련해보는 것도 좋겠네요!

Review – **지금까지 배운 요소를 구분하는 연습**

1. 여기는 처음부터 빠르게 변환하려고 하지 말고, 문장 속의 요소를 구분하는 연습이 필요해요. 한 문장씩 차근차근 읽어보고, 영어로 어떻게 말하는지 생각해보고, 천천히 말하는 연습을 해요.
2. 쓰면서 다시 생각해보는 연습을 해요.
3. 답을 확인해 보아요.

Dialogue Practice – **실제 상황에서의 응용**

1. 영어를 먼저 읽어보아요!
2. 문장을 보면서 이게 배운 것 중에서 어떤 부분에 해당되는지 생각해봐요! (want to 인지, have to 인지 등등) 이렇게 구분만 할 수 있어도 너무 좋아요!
3. 영어가 익숙해지면, 뒤 페이지에 있는 한국어를 보며 입으로 영작에 도전해 보아요!

힌트와 하이라이트의 활용

힌트가 있는 문항이 있어요. 힌트를 보고 문장을 만들어요. 영어 문장을 떠올리는데도 도움되고, 적을 때는 스펠링도 도움이 되어서, 단어를 직접 찾아보는데 시간을 소요할 필요가 없어요!
하이라이트는 급하게 가지 말고, '잠깐!' 생각해 보라는 거예요! 조금 주의해야 답을 찾을 수 있으니, 하이라이트 부분은 별표를 하고 자세히 봐주세요!

목차

Unit ·—————————————

0

시작하기
불규칙 동사 과거형

불규칙 동사란?

주로 동작, 움직임이 들어간 단어로,
우리말의 먹다, 마시다, 가다, 일하다 등에 해당되는 단어예요.

한국어에서 과거를 표현할 때는 주로 'ㅆ'을 붙이고 [먹다 - 먹었다], 미래를 표현할 때는 'ㄹ'을 붙이는 [먹다-먹을 거다] 패턴을 가지는 것처럼, 영어에서도 그런 패턴이 있어요. 하지만, 그 패턴을 따라가지 않는 (즉, 규칙적이지 않은) 동사를 **불규칙 동사**라고 합니다.

이거 정말 너무 중요해요! 그래서, 저와 함께 외워볼 건데요! 무언가를 외우는 방법은요, 구구단처럼 입으로 반복해서 외우는 게 효과가 제일 좋아요.
저와 함께 강의를 소리로 들으면서, 말로 따라 하다 보면, 금방 외워지고 익숙해질 거예요!

원형	과거	과거분사P.P.	원형	과거	과거분사P.P.
be	was / were	been	leave	left	left
become	became	become	lend	lent	lent
begin	began	begun	let	let	let
bite	bit	bitten	lose	lost	lost
blow	blew	blown	make	made	made
break	broke	broken	mean	meant	meant
bring	brought	brought	meet	met	met
build	built	built	pay	paid	paid
buy	bought	bought	put	put	put
catch	caught	caught	read	read [red]	read [red]
choose	chose	chosen	ride	rode	ridden
come	came	come	ring	rang	rung
cost	cost	cost	run	ran	run
cut	cut	cut	say	said	said
do	did	done	see	saw	seen
drink	drank	drunk	sell	sold	sold
drive	drove	driven	send	sent	sent
eat	ate	eaten	sing	sang	sung
fall	fell	fallen	sit	sat	sat
feel	felt	felt	sleep	slept	slept
find	found	found	speak	spoke	spoken
fly	flew	flown	spend	spent	spent
forget	forgot	forgotten	stand	stood	stood
get	got	got	steal	stole	stolen
give	gave	given	swim	swam	swum
go	went	gone/been	take	took	taken
grow	grew	grown	teach	taught	taught
hang	hung	hung	tell	told	told
have	had	had	think	thought	thought
hide	hid	hidden	throw	threw	thrown
hit	hit	hit	understand	understood	understood
hold	held	held	wake	woke	woken
hurt	hurt	hurt	wear	wore	worn
keep	kept	kept	win	won	won
know	knew	known	write	wrote	written

Unit

1

'지금' 하고 있는 것을 말하고 싶을 때

am / is / are + -ing '지금 ~ 해'

'지금' 하는 일이나, 벌어지고 있는 상황을 표현할 때 쓰는 'am, is, are + -ing'는
'현재' 파트예요. 이 형식의 문장에는 '시간'이라는 요소가 이미 들어가 있어서,
now를 따로 사용하지 않아도, '지금' 일어나는 일을 나타내요.
생활에서는 '지금 집에 가고 있어', '밥 먹고 있어' 등, 무언가를 '하고 있어'라고
많이 표현하지만, 짧게 '지금 집에 가', '지금 밥 먹어'와 같이 이야기하기도 해요.
짧은 '~해'에 지금 무언갈 하고 있다는 의미가 담겨 있는 셈이죠.

Positive (긍정)		Negative (부정)		Question (의문)	
I am -ing		I am not -ing		Am I -ing?	
He She It	is -ing	He She It	isn't -ing	Is	he she it	-ing?
You We They	are -ing	You We They	aren't -ing	Are	you we they	-ing?
~ 해 (지금) ~ 하고 있어		~ 안 해 (지금) ~ 안 하고 있어 / 하고 있지 않아		~ 해? (지금) ~ 하고 있어?	

이렇게 만듭니다!

Be동사 현재의 'am, is, are'에, 문장의 핵심인 동사를 '-ing' 형태로 붙여 주면 돼요!

Positive (긍정)	Negative (부정)	Question (의문)
나 지금 집에 가. I am going home (now).	나 지금 집에 안 가. I am not going home (now).	너 지금 집에 가? Are you going home (now)?

<주의할 점>

동사에 '-ing'를 붙이면, 더 이상 동사라고 부르지 않고, 명사화 되어서 '동명사'라고 불려요! 따라서 문장에 동사(be 동사)가 또 따로 필요한 거예요. 그래서 'ing'는 'be'동사와 절친이에요.

<함께 쓰는 단어>

시제에는 '시간'이라는 요소가 있기 때문에, 자주 함께 쓰는 단어가 있어요:

now, at the moment, at present.

<스펠링 법칙>

단어가 -e 로 끝나는 단어에 ing를 붙일 때는, e를 떼고 ing를 붙입니다. E가 있으면 발음하기가 불편하거든요!

예: make -> making [메이크 -> 메이크잉(X), 메이킹(O)]

정답확인 : P 254

01	우리 지금 영어 공부해.	
02	나 지금 일하는데. 내가 나중에 전화해도 될까?	
03	그 애 지금 열심히 공부하고 있어.	열심히 공부하다 study hard
04	우리 지금 집에 가.	
05	Sally 지금 오고 있어.	
06	나 지금 뭔가 만들고 있어.	
07	우리 지금 공항에 가.	운전해서 가다 drive to, 공항 the airport
08	우리 지금 너 기다리고 있어.	기다리다 wait for
09	쉬! 얘 지금 자.	쉬! Shush!
10	나 지금 샤워하는데. 금방 나갈게.	

11	너 늦게(까지) 일하네. 🔊	
12	조금 배가 고파진다. 너는? 🔊	배가 고파지다 get hungry
13	나 지금 점심 먹는데, 같이 먹을래? 🔊	같이 하다/같이 먹다 join
14	우리 지금 나가. 전화 끊어야 돼. 🔊	전화 끊다 hang up
15	그 애 거짓말 하는거야. 🔊	거짓말하다 lie - lying
16	그 애 지금 재미있게 놀고 있어. 🔊	재미있게 놀다 have fun
17	미안, 제가 지금 운전 중이에요. 나중에 **전화할게요.** 🔊	
18	나 지금 핸드폰 게임해. 재미있어. 🔊	핸드폰 게임하다 play a game on my phone
19	우리 지금 뭔가 하고 있어서. 이거 내가 나중에 **해도 될 까?** 🔊	
20	(나) 농담하는 거야. 🔊	농담하다 joke/kid

21	누군가 여기 앉아요(여기 자리있어요). 이거 가져가면 안 돼요. 🔊	누군가 = 주인공, sit-sitting
22	나 지금 내 핸드폰 찾아. 🔊	찾다, 찾아보다 look for
23	저 이런거 찾는데요. 어디 있어요? 🔊	이런거 something like this
24	나 사진들 보고 있어. 내가 좋은 거 보여줄게. 🔊	보다 look at, 좋은거 a good one
25	전화 온다. 🔊	전화가 주인공! (전화)오다, 울리다 ring
26	잠깐만. 나 지금 뭔가 생각하고 있어. 🔊	
27	나 그거 듣는 건데. 그냥 켜 놔줄래? 🔊	듣다 listen to, 켜 놓다 leave-on
28	노력하고 있어. 그거 오늘까지 끝낼거야. 🔊	노력하다 try/try hard
29	너 오늘 멋져 보여! 🔊	멋져보이다 look good
30	우린 모든 걸 해보고있어. 우린 최선을 다하고 있어. 🔊	해보다 try, 최선을 다하다 try one's best/do one's best [one's= 소유격, 예: my, his, your, our 등]

긍정문 am, is, are -ing

☞ 오른쪽 힌트를 이용해서, 직접 문장을 만들어보세요!

31	지금 비 와.	시작이 애매할땐! "It"
32	밖에 눈 와. 너무 아름다워.	
33	(점점) 나아지고 있어.	나아지다 get better
34	(점점) 추워진다. 너 따뜻해?	추워지다 get cold
35	(점점) 나빠져.	나빠지다 get worse
36	어두워진다. 우리 지금 가는 게 좋을 것 같아.	어두워지다 get dark
37	늦어진다. 나 지금 나갈게.	늦어지다 get late
38	이거 (점점) 더 커져. 어떡하지? [=내가 뭘 할까?]	더 커지다 get bigger
39	(점점) 더 어려워져.	더 어려워지다 get harder
40	이거 돼.	되다, 작동하다 work

부정문 am, is, are not-ing

☞ 오른쪽 힌트를 이용해서, 직접 문장을 만들어보세요!

41	나 그거 지금 안 봐(TV). 그거 꺼도 돼.	
42	우리 지금 아무데도 안 가.	
43	나 지금 아무것도 안 해. 만날래?	
44	나 이거 지금 안 써. 너 써도 돼.	
45	아무도 여기 앉지 않아요. 이거 가져가도 돼요.	아무도=주인공! 아무도 nobody
46	나 우는거 아니야. 내 눈이 아파.	울다 cry, 아픈 sore
47	이 펜 안 나와. (=안 돼)	나오다, 되다 work
48	나 지금 안 자.	
49	나 지금 일 안해. 통화할 수 있어.	통화하다 talk
50	나 오늘 일 안해. 쉬는 날이야.	쉬는 날 one's day off

부정문 am, is, are not-ing

☞ 오른쪽 힌트를 이용해서, 직접 문장을 만들어보세요!

51	우리 아무도 기다리고 있지 않아.	
52	나 그거 혼자 하는거 아니야. 내 친구들이 도와주고 있어.	
53	나 지금 운전 중 아니야.	
54	우리 네 얘기 하는거 아니야.	~에 대해 얘기하다 talk about
55	나 아무것도 계획하고 있지 않아.	plan-planning
56	나 농담하는 거 아니야. 나 진지해.	진지한, 심각한 serious
57	지금 더 이상 비 안 와. 그리고 이제 비 안 올거야. 우산 안 가져가도 돼.	
58	지금 눈 안 오는데.	
59	이거 안 돼.	
60	그거 나아지고 있지 않아. 우리 그거에 대해 뭔가 해야돼.	

의문문 Are you -ing?

☞ 오른쪽 힌트를 이용해서, 직접 문장을 만들어보세요!

61	너 지금 뭔가 하고 있니? 바쁘니?	(뭔가 하느라)바쁜 busy
62	지금 뭐 해?	
63	지금 어디 가는 거야? 나도 **가도 돼?**	
64	지금 어딘가 가는 길이니? 바쁘니?	바쁜, 서둘러야 되는 in a hurry
65	너 내말 듣고 있는거야?	듣다 listen to
66	왜 웃어?	웃다 laugh
67	뭐 보고 있어? 그게 뭐야?	보다 look at
68	너 뭐 찾고 있어?	찾다, 찾아보다 look for
69	뭔가 찾니? 이거니?	
70	누구 찾으세요? (누구 바꿔줄까요? / 누구 불러줄까요?)	

71	너 왜 날 그렇게 쳐다보니? 그만해! (Stop it!) 🔊	쳐다보다 look at, 그렇게 like that
72	너 뭔가 먹고 있니? 뭐 먹어? 🔊	
73	지금 저녁 요리해? 뭐 요리해? 🔊	
74	무슨 생각하고 있니? 🔊	
75	누군가 기다리니? 🔊	
76	너 왜 울어? (너)괜찮아? (너)아파? 🔊	
77	무슨 말이에요? (뭘 말하는 거예요?) 🔊	말하다 say / talk about
78	지금 이거 쓰는 거예요? 제가 이거 빌려도 되나요? 🔊	
79	지금 이 자리 맡아 놓는 거예요? 🔊	맡아 놓다 save, 이 자리 this seat
80	지금 오고 있어? 어디야? 🔊	

의문문 Are you -ing?

☞ 오른쪽 힌트를 이용해서, 직접 문장을 만들어보세요!

81	너 지금 장난해?	장난하다, 농담하다 joke/kid
82	그 애 지금 뭐 해? 일해?	
83	이거(TV) 너 지금 보는 거야? 아님 내가 꺼도 돼?	
84	너 누구랑 이야기 하는거야? 혼잣말 하는 거야?	혼잣말 하다 talk to oneself [oneself=myself, yourself 등]
85	너 뭐 입고 있어?	
86	우리 지금 어디 가는 거야?	
87	너 기분 좀 나아? 기분 어때?	기분이 낫다 feel better, 기분이 들다 feel
88	내가 지금 여기서 뭐 하는 거지?	
89	뭘 기다리는 거야? 그냥 해!	그냥 해! Just do it! / Go for it!
90	뭐 하려고? (=뭐 하려고 하는 거야?)	하려고 하다, 시도하다 try to do

의문문 Is it -ing?

☞ 오른쪽 힌트를 이용해서, 직접 문장을 만들어보세요!

91	비가 또 와? 🔊	
92	밖에 눈오니? 🔊	
93	그거 되니? 🔊	
94	나아지고 있니? 🔊	
95	그거 (점점) 커져? 🔊	
96	더 쉬워지고 있어? 🔊	더 쉬워지다 get easier
97	그거 깜빡여? 켜져 있어? 🔊	깜빡이다 blink, 켜 있는 on
98	이게 왜 깜빡이는 거지? 뭔가 잘못됐나? 🔊	뭔가=주인공, 잘못된 wrong
99	이게 왜 삐삐거리지? 이것 좀 봐줄래? 🔊	삐삐거리다 beep, 보다 have a look (at)/take a look (at)
100	이게 왜 이렇게 오래 걸리는 거지? 🔊	(시간이)걸리다 take, 이렇게 오래 so long/this long

복습강의 MP3

Positive (긍정)		Negative (부정)		Question (의문)	
I want to	~할래, 하고 싶어	I don't want to	~안 할래	Do you want to?	~할래?
I have to	~해야 돼 (의무)	I don't have to	~안 해도 돼	Do I have to?	~해야 돼?
I can	~할수있어	I can't	~못 해, 할 수 없어	Can you?	~할 수 있어? ~해줄래? (부탁)
You can	~해도 돼 (허락)	You can't	~하면 안 돼	Can I?	~해도 돼?
I will	~할게	I won't	~안 할게	Shall I?	~할까? (제안)
I should	~하는 게 좋겠다	I shouldn't	~안 하는 게 좋겠다	Should I?	~하는 게 좋을까?
I think I should	~하는 게 좋을 것 같아	I don't think I should	~안 하는 게 좋을 것 같아	Do you think I should?	~하는 게 좋을 것 같아?
I'd like to	~하고 싶어요	I wouldn't like to	~하고 싶지 않아요	Would you like to?	~하실래요?
I'm going to	~할 거야	I'm not going to	~안 할 거야	Are you going to?	~할거야?
I am -ing	해, 하고있어 (지금)	I'm not -ing	안 해, 안하고있어	Are you -ing?	해? (지금) 하고 있어?

01	나 이거 빌려야 돼.	17	저 뭐 빌려야 되나요?
02	너 이거 빌려도 돼.	18	나 이거 빌리는 게 좋을까?
03	이거 빌릴래요? 난 괜찮은데.	19	너 이게 왜 빌리고 싶어?
04	저 이거 빌리고 싶어요.	20	내가 어느거 빌릴까?
05	너 이거 빌리면 안 돼.	21	너 이거 왜 빌려야 돼?
06	나 이거 빌릴게. 고마워.	22	넌 내가 어느 걸 빌리는 게 좋을 것 같아?
07	나 이거 빌리는 게 좋겠어.	23	너 이거 안 빌리는 게 좋겠다.
08	나 이거 빌릴 수 있어.	24	나 내 친구한테 책 빌리고 있어. [언제?, ~한테 from]
09	나 이거 빌리기 싫어.	25	나 그 애한테 돈 빌리는거 아니야. (지금)
10	우리 이거 빌릴까?	26	너 그걸 왜 그 애한테 빌려? (지금)
11	너 이거 안 빌려도 돼. 내가 빌려줄 수 있어.		
12	우리 이거 못 빌려. 사야 돼.		
13	저 이거 빌려야 되나요?		
14	너 이거 빌릴 수 있어?		
15	이거 안 빌릴거야.		
16	어느거 빌릴래? 너가 골라도 돼.		

정답확인 : P 256

A: Excuse me, are you travelling alone?

B: Yes, I am travelling alone. Why are you asking?

A: We are travelling together. Can you change/switch seats (with us)?

B: Ok. Where is your seat?

A: It is 8E. You are so/very/really kind. Thank you so much.

A: Can I have your tickets and passports, please?

B: Here you are/ Here they are.

A: Are you (guys/two) travelling together?

B: Yes, we are travelling together. Can we sit together?

A: Hang on. I will check. / Let me check.

B: It is a long flight. We really want to sit together(, please).

A: Yes, you can sit together. Can you put your bags here (, please)?

A: Here are my ticket and my passport. / These are my ticket and passport. I am travelling with a/my friend. Can we check in together?

B: Sure. Where is your friend?

A: He is there. I will call him.

B: Do you (guys/two) want to sit together? / Would you like to sit together?

A: Yes, please. Is it possible?

B: Hold on. Unfortunately, you can't sit together.

A: It is ok, then.

기내

A : 실례지만, 혼자 여행하시는 건가요? [언제?? - 지금!!]

B : 네, 혼자 여행하는 거예요. 왜 물어보시나요?

A : 저희 같이 여행하는데요. 자리 바꿔 주실 수 있어요?

B : 알았어요. 당신의 자리가 어디예요?

A : 8E예요. 너무 친절하세요. 감사해요.

공항

A : 티켓하고 여권 주세요.

B : 여기요.

A : 두 분 같이 여행하시는 건가요?

B : 네, 저희 둘이 같이 여행하는 거예요. 저희 같이 앉을 수 있나요?

A : 잠시만요, 확인해 볼게요.

B : 오랜 비행인데요. [오랜 비행 a long flight] 저희 정말 같이 앉고 싶어요.

A : 네, 같이 앉을 수 있어요. 여기에 가방을 올려 주실래요?

A: 여기 티켓하고 여권이요. 저 친구랑 같이 여행하는데요. 같이 체크인 해도 되나요?

B: 물론이죠. 친구 분은 어디 있죠?

A: 저기요. 제가 부를게요.

B: 두 분 같이 앉고 싶으신가요?

A: 네. 가능한가요?

B: 잠시만요. 불행히도, 같이 앉을 수 없네요.

A: 괜찮아요 그럼.

공항

A: Excuse me, can I ask you something?

B: Yes/Sure, what can I do (for you)?

A: This is my boarding pass. Where do I have to go?

B: You have to go to Gate 4. I am going there now. I will show you.

—

A: Are you looking for something?

B: Yes, I am looking for Gate 4. Can you help me?

A: Sure/Of course. Can you show me your pass? / Can I see your pass?

B: This is my pass.

A: It is this way. You have to follow this green line. Then, it is on your right/on the right. It's easy to find.

A: What is that?

B: It is a hole.

A: It is pretty/quite big.

B: It is getting bigger. This is my favorite sweater. It is really warm and comfortable.

A: That's a shame.

B: It is almost 7. It is getting late.

A: Is it already 7? I think we should leave now.

A: 실례지만, 뭔가 물어봐도 되나요?

B: 네, 제가 뭘 할 수 있죠?

A: 이제 제 보딩 패스인데요. 어디로 가야 하나요?

B: 4번 게이트로 가야 돼요. 저도 지금 거기 가는데요. 제가 보여줄게요.

—

A: 뭔가 찾고 있어요?

B: 네, 저 4번 게이트 찾고 있는데요. 도와주실래요?

A: 당연하죠. 당신의 탑승권 보여줄래요?

B: 이게 제 탑승권이에요.

A: 이쪽이에요. 이 초록색 선 [this green line]을 따라가야 돼요. 그리고, 오른쪽[on the right/on your right]에 있어요. 찾기 쉬워요.

A: 그게 뭐야?

B: 구멍[a hole]이야.

A: 꽤 큰데.

B: 점점 커져. 이거 내가 가장 좋아하는[my favorite] 스웨터인데.

정말 따뜻하고 편해.

A: 안됐다 (안타깝다). [That's a shame!]

B: 거의[almost] 7시다. 늦어지고 있어.

A: 벌써 7시야? 우리 지금 출발하는 게 좋을 것 같네.

Unit

2

'원래' 하는 걸 말하고 싶을 때

'원래' 하는 걸 말하고 싶을 때

동사 현재형 '(원래) ~ 해'

주인공(주어) 다음에 바로 동사를 넣으면, 주어가 '원래' 하는 것을 표현할 수 있는 현재형이에요. 예를 들어, '지금 밥을 먹어'는 '지금' 하는 것이라 'am/is/are -ing'를 사용하지만, '난 밥을 일찍 먹어 (원래!)', 혹은 '난 아침 안 먹어 (원래!)' 이런 표현에는 -ing를 넣지 않고, 동사를 바로 넣으면 돼요!

'원래' 하는 건, '난 공부를 언제 어디서 해, 난 -를 좋아해, 그 애는 어디에 살아, 여기는 비가 자주 와'등, 지금 당장 일어나는 일이 아니라, 기존의 사실, 잘 변하지 않는 진실 등을 표현해요.

Positive (긍정)		Negative (부정)		Question (의문)		
I We You They	go like	I We You They	don't	Do	I we you they	?
He She It	goes likes	He She It	doesn't	Does	he she it	?
~해 (원래)		~ 안 해 (원래)		~해? (원래)		

주인공이 3인칭 단수(**3인칭 = 나, 너를 제외한 다른 사람 혹은 물건/단수 = 한 명, 한 개**)인 경우에는 **동사 뒤에 -s를 붙여줘야 돼요!**

부정문이나 의문문은, **이미** don't에 **-(e)s를 붙여서** doesn't으로 사용하고, do에 -(e)s를 붙여서 does를 사용하므로, 동사는 편하게 원형으로 사용하면 돼요!!

- 주인공이 'I'이면 동사가 바로 나오면 되고, he/she/it 같은 3인칭 단수이면 동사에 –s를 붙여주면 돼요!

- 부정문에서는 don't/doesn't 뒤에 바로 동사 원형 넣고, 의문문에서도 Do/Does 사용하고 동사 원형 넣으면 돼요!

  (부정문의 don't나, 의문문의 do는, '하다'라는 의미를 가진 동사가 아니라, '현재'의 부정이나 의문을 표시해서, 동사가 꼭! 따로 필요해요!!!)

Positive (긍정)	Negative (부정)	Question (의문)
난 서울에 살아. I live in Seoul.	난 서울에 안 살아. I don't live in Seoul.	넌 어디에 살아? Where do you live?
그 애는 이걸 좋아해. He likes it	그 앤 이걸 안 좋아해. He doesn't like it.	그 앤 뭘 좋아해? What does he like?

<함께 쓰는 단어>

우리는 무언가를 '항상/가끔/자주/매일' 한다고 말하기 때문에, 이 단어들과 자주 함께 써요:

always, usually, often, sometimes, hardly ever, never, every day

<스펠링 법칙>

1. –o / -ch/ -sh로 끝나는 단어는 –es 예: goes, does, watches, washes

2. –y 로 끝나는 단어

    ① 모음(a,e,i,o,u) + y : 는 그냥 –s 붙입니다 [예: stays, pays]

    ② 자음 + y : y 떼고 –ies [예: studies, tries, cries]

3. 불규칙 : have -> has

긍정문 I 동사 / He 동사s
☞ 오른쪽 힌트를 이용해서, 직접 문장을 만들어보세요!

훈련용 MP3

정답확인 : P 257

01	우리 이거 필요해. 우리 이거 가져도 돼?	필요하다 need
02	저 도움이 필요해요.	도움 help
03	이해해요. 설명하지 않아도 돼요.	
04	그 애는 날 이해해줘.	
05	난 보통 7시에 일어나. I usually	보통 usually, 빈도부사[빈도/횟수 표현 단어]는 일반동사 앞! (& be 동사 뒤!)
06	그 애는 항상 일찍 일어나. He always	항상, 늘 always
07	나는 보통 12시에 자.	자다 go to bed
08	그 애는 항상 잠을 늦게 자.	
09	난 동물 좋아해.	좋아하다 like, 동물 animals
10	Tom은 이거 좋아해.	

긍정문 I 동사 / He 동사s
☞ 오른쪽 힌트를 이용해서, 직접 문장을 만들어보세요!

11	난 이게 더 좋아.	더 좋아하다, 선호하다 prefer
12	Tom은 커피를 더 좋아해.	
13	난 이게 싫어.	싫어하다 hate
14	Jim은 이거 싫어해.	
15	이 가게는 9시에 열고, 6시에 닫아.	이 가게=주인공!
16	난 이미 알아.	이미, 벌써 already
17	Jim도 알고있어.	
18	나 그거 있어.	있다, 가지고 있다 have
19	그 애 차(자동차) 있어.	
20	우리 그거 할 시간 있어.	동사를 두 개 넣고 싶으면?? "to"!!

긍정문 I 동사 / He 동사s

☞ 오른쪽 힌트를 이용해서, 직접 문장을 만들어보세요!

21	난 서울에 살고, 엄마는 경기도에 살아.	살다 live (in)
22	나 그거 진심이야.	진심이다, 뜻하다, 의미하다 mean
23	나 그거 기억나.	
24	그 애는 모든 걸 다 기억해.	
25	난 그게 그리워.	그리워하다, 보고싶다 miss
26	그 애는 항상 그래.	
27	나 거기 일주일에 한 번 가.	일주일에 한 번 once a week
28	그 애 거기에 매일 다녀.	
29	저희 신용카드 받아요.	받다 take/accept
30	그 가게에서 양말도 팔아. 거기서 양말 살 수 있어.	팔다 sell

긍정문 It 동사s

☞ 오른쪽 힌트를 이용해서, 직접 문장을 만들어보세요!

31	여기 비 많이 와.	많이 a lot
32	이거 아파.	아프다 hurt
33	이거 돼.	되다, 작동하다 work
34	이거 쉽게 깨져. 조심해야 돼.	깨지다 break, 쉽게 easily
35	그거 오래 걸려.	시간이 걸리다 take
36	그거 돈 많이 들어.	돈이 들다 cost
37	여기 오는데 한 시간 걸려.	
38	그거 설치하는데 돈 많이 들어.	
39	그거 좋아 보여.	보이다 look
40	그거 비싸 보여.	

Speaking Practice

⏱ 1min

부정문 I don't / He doesn't

☞ 오른쪽 힌트를 이용해서, 직접 문장을 만들어보세요!

41	기억이 안나. 🔊	
42	그 앤 아직 몰라. 🔊	
43	난 그 애가 이해 안 돼. 🔊	
44	제 친구는 김치 안 먹어요. 그 애한테 너무 매워. 🔊	
45	너 이거 필요없어. 안 사도 돼. 🔊	
46	난 술 안 마셔. 🔊	
47	Jack은 담배 안 펴. 🔊	
48	전 이거 안 좋아해요. 🔊	
49	그 애 티비 (원래) 안 봐. 🔊	
50	우린 거기 잘 안 가요. 🔊	잘??? '잘한다'는 의미 or '자주' 의 의미??

기초영어 1000문장 말하기 연습 2

부정문 I don't / He doesn't

☞ 오른쪽 힌트를 이용해서, 직접 문장을 만들어보세요!

51	나 지금 현찰이 없어. 🔊	없다 = 가지고 있지 않다
52	저 지금 시간이 없어요. 🔊	
53	거기 갈 시간이 없어. 🔊	동사를 더 넣고 싶으면??
54	우리 그럴 시간 없어. 🔊	
55	그 앤 시간이 없어. 그 앤 바빠. 🔊	
56	나 그거 진심이 아니에요. 미안. 🔊	진심이다, 뜻하다 mean
57	그거 상관없어. 🔊	상관 있다 matter
58	이거 안 돼요. 🔊	
59	오래 안 걸려요. 🔊	시간이 걸리다 take
60	돈 별로 안 들어. 🔊	돈이 들다 cost, 별로 much

의문문 Do you? / Does he?

☞ 오른쪽 힌트를 이용해서, 직접 문장을 만들어보세요!

61	이거 좋아해? 뭘 좋아해? 🔊	
62	Jenny는 이거 좋아해? 🔊	
63	넌 그 앨 믿어? 난 그 앨 **못** 믿겠어. 🔊	
64	그 앤 뭘 원하는 거야? 🔊	
65	어디 살아요? 🔊	
66	어디서 일해? 🔊	
67	Jack은 어디서 일해? 🔊	
68	넌 뭐해? (원래) 🔊	원래 뭐하냐고 하면 = 직업을 물어보는 말이에요!
69	그 앤 뭐해? (원래) 🔊	
70	몇 시에 일 끝나요? (=몇 시 퇴근해요?) 🔊	

71	거기 자주 가니?	
72	너희는 몇 시에 닫아요? (=몇 시까지 하세요?)	
73	그 사람 자주 보니? 얼마나 자주 봐?	얼마나 자주 how often
74	Sam도 알고 있어?	
75	넌 어떻게 (뭘) 생각해?	어떻게 (뭘) what : 생각이 뭔지 묻는것이라 how가 아니라 what! How=어떻게 하는지 방법을 물음
76	어느게 더 좋아?	더 좋아하다, 선호하다 prefer
77	이거 필요해? 나 이거 너한테 주고 싶어.	
78	(저) 어느게 필요해요?	
79	넌 내가 미워? 왜 날 미워해?	미워하다, 싫어하다 hate
80	나 보고 싶어?	보고싶다, 그리워하다 miss

의문문 Do you?

☞ 오른쪽 힌트를 이용해서, 직접 문장을 만들어보세요!

81	(너) 무슨 말(뜻)이에요?	뜻하다, 의미하다 mean
82	그게 무슨 뜻이에요?	그거=주인공
83	너 진심이야? 너 심각해?	진심이다, 뜻하다 mean, 심각한, 진지한 serious
84	그래서, 너 나한테 원하는 게 뭐야?	~한테, 부터 from
85	나 어때 보여? (나) 괜찮아 보여?	보이다 look
86	시간 있어?	있다, 가지고 있다 have
87	여기 올 시간 있어?	
88	나랑 통화할 시간 있어?	통화하다 talk
89	저 화장실 갈 시간 있나요?	
90	공부할 시간 있니? 난 아무것도 할 시간이 없는데.	

의문문 Does it?

☞ 오른쪽 힌트를 이용해서, 직접 문장을 만들어보세요!

91	(그게) 상관있나요? (=중요한가요?) 🔊	
92	**그거 돼?** 🔊	
93	그거 아파? 🔊	
94	**그거 쉽게 깨져?** 🔊	
95	그런 일 자주 있어? 🔊	무슨 일이 생기다, 일어나다 happen
96	**그거 (사이즈) 맞아?** 🔊	(사이즈가) 맞다 fit
97	그거 오래 걸려? 🔊	
98	**그거 얼마나 오래 걸려?** 🔊	
99	거기 가는데 얼마나 오래 걸려? 🔊	
100	**그거 얼마 들어요?** 🔊	

Positive (긍정)		Negative (부정)		Question (의문)	
I am -ing	해, 하고있어 (지금)	I'm not -ing	안 해, 안하고있어	Are you -ing?	해? (지금) 하고 있어?
I 동사	해 (원래)	I don't	안 해	Do you?	해? (원래)

01	우리 뭐 볼까?	17	난 네가 이거 안 보는 게 좋을 것 같아. 무서워. [무서운 scary]
02	이거 볼래?	18	이거 나랑 봐줄래?
03	나 그거 봐야 돼.	19	나도 봐도 돼?
04	나 이거 보기 싫어.	20	넌 우리가 어느 걸 보는 게 좋을 것 같니?
05	뭐 볼래요?	21	나 지금 그거 보는 건데. 채널 바꾸면 안 돼.
06	너 이거 봐도 돼.	22	너 뭐 볼 거야?
07	내가 그거 이따가 볼게.	23	난 티비 잘 안 봐.
08	나 이거 지금 안 봐도 돼.	24	그 앤 티비 맨날 봐.
09	넌 이거 보면 안 돼. 넌 너무 어려.	25	너 지금 뭐 봐?
10	나 그거 보는 게 좋을까?	26	나 그거 지금 안 봐. 꺼도 돼.
11	나 이거 보고 싶어.	27	너 티비보니? 보통 뭘 봐?
12	우리 이번엔 이 영화로 보는 게 좋겠어.	28	나 그 영화 다음주에 볼 거야.
13	나 이거 안 볼게.		
14	나 이거 못 봐. 난 공포영화 안 좋아해. [공포영화 horror movies]		
15	우리 뭐 보는 게 좋을까?		
16	저 이거 봐야 되나요?		

정답확인 : P 260

숙박시설 (숙소)

A: Do you have (any) rooms available? / Do you have (any) available rooms?

B: I am sorry. We don't have (any) rooms available. / We don't have (any) available rooms. We are fully booked today.

A: Do you know (any) other places?

B: I will make a (phone) call.

A: Thank you so much.

B: I think you should go to Four Seasons. They have (some) rooms available. / They have (some) available rooms.

A: Where is that?

B: It is 5 minutes away from here.

—

A: We need a room for two (people). Do you have it/a room/ rooms?

B: Let me check. Yes, We have a/one room. Do you want it? / Would you like it?

A: Yes, please. How much is it to stay a night/for a(the) night?

B: It is Saturday today. So, It is 90 dollars.

A: How much is it to stay for two nights? Is it 180?

B: No, it is 160. Do you want to stay (here) for two nights?

A: I will think about it, and I will let you know tomorrow. / I will think about it and let you know tomorrow. Do I have to pay now?

B: No. But we need your credit card details. Can I have your credit card(, please)?

A: Here you are. / Here it is.

A: (너희) 이용 가능한[available] 방 있어요?

B: 미안해요. 우리 이용 가능한 방이 없어요. [=가지고 있지 않아요] 우린 오늘 예약이 꽉 찼어요. [예약이 꽉찬 fully booked]

A: 다른 곳들 [other places] 아시나요?

B: 전화 한 통 해볼게요.

A: 감사해요.

B: 포시즌스에 가는 게 좋을 것 같아요. 그들은 이용 가능한 방이 있어요.

A: 그게 어딘가요?

B: 여기서 5분 떨어져[away] 있어요.

—

A: 저희 두 명을 위한 방이 필요한데요. 방이 있나요?

B: 체크해볼게요. [Let me check.] 네, 저희 방이 하나 있네요. 그걸 원하시나요?

A: 네. 하룻밤 동안 머무는데 얼마예요?

B: 오늘이 토요일이라서, 90불이에요.

A: 두 밤 머무르는데는 얼마예요. 180인가요?

B: 아니요, 160이에요. 두 밤 머물래요?

A: 생각해 볼게요. 그리고, 내일 아침에 알려드릴게요. 지금 계산해야 되나요?

B: 아니요. 하지만, 우리는 당신의 신용카드 정보가 필요해요. 신용카드 주세요.

A: 여기요.

A: I need a room for two (people). Do you have it/a room/ rooms?

B: I am sorry. We don't have (any) single rooms. We have (some) double rooms available. / We have (some) available double rooms.

A: How much is it per night?

B: It is 95 dollars per night.

A: How much is the single room per night?

B: It is 70 (dollars per night).

A: Can I use the double room (for) tonight, and (can I) change to /have the single room tomorrow?

B: Yes, you can (do that).

A: Ok, then. / Then, I will take/have the double room(,please).

—

A: Do you have a room/rooms for 3 people?

B: Yes, we do. / Yes, we have a room/rooms.

A: How much is it per person?

B: It is 40 dollars per person.

A: Does the room have ocean views?

B: No (, it doesn't). It has garden views.

숙박시설 (숙소)

A: 저 싱글룸이 필요한데, 이용 가능한 싱글룸이 있나요?

B: 미안해요 싱글룸은 없고요, 이용 가능한 더블룸은 있어요

A: 하룻밤 당 [per night] 얼마예요?

B: 밤 당 95불이에요.

A: 하룻밤 당 싱글룸은 얼마예요?

B: 70불이에요.

A: 오늘밤은 더블룸 사용하고, 내일 싱글룸으로 바꿔도 되나요?

B: 네, 그렇게 해도 돼요.

A: 그럼, 오늘밤은 더블룸으로 할게요. [하다 take]

—

A: 세 명을 위한 방이 있나요?

B: 네, 방 있어요.

A: 한 사람 당 [per person] 얼마예요?

B: 한 사람 당 40불이에요.

A: 그 방이 바다 전망을 가지고 있나요?

B: 아니요. 가든 전망을 가지고 있어요.

Unit

3

예측이나 예상을 말하고 싶을 때

예측이나 예상을 말하고 싶을 때

will '~할 걸(아마 그럴 걸), 할 거야'

현재나 미래상황에 대해 예측이나 예상의 의미로 '~할 걸(아마 그럴 걸),' 혹은 '~할 거야'라고 말하고 싶을 때, 'will'을 사용해요.

이런 예측이나 예상은 화자의 생각이 담긴 경우가 많기 때문에, 'think'와도 너무 잘 어울려요.

Positive (긍정)	Negative (부정)	Question (의문)
I will	I won't	Will you?
~할 걸, 할 거야	~안 할 걸, 안 할 거야	~할까? [예측]
I think { I / we / you / they / he / she / it } will	I don't think { I / we / you / they / he / she / it } will	Do you think { I / we / you / they / he / she / it } will
~할 것 같아	~안 할 것 같아	~할 것 같아?

이렇게 만듭니다!

문장의 핵심단어인 '동사'를 넣습니다!

Positive (긍정)	Negative (부정)	Question (의문)
그 애가 이해할 거야. He will understand.	그 애 이해하지 않을 거야. He won't understand.	그 애가 이해할까? Will he understand?
나도 갈 것 같아. I think I will go, too.	난 안 갈 것 같아. I don't think I will go.	넌 갈 것 같아? Do you think you will go?

<심화 표현>

시간을 더 다채롭게 표현할 때 쓸 수 있는 'if/when/as soon as/ before/after/until'을 'will' 과 함께 사용할 수 있어요.

if ~하면 (만일)			내가 거기 가면 (혹시, 만약),
when ~하면	if when as soon as after before until	I go there,	내가 거기 가면,
as soon as ~하자마자			내가 거기 가자마자,
after ~하고 나서, 한 후에			내가 거기 간 후에,
before ~하기 전에			내가 거기 가기 전에,
until ~할 때까지			내가 거기 갈 때까지,

예: 내가 거기 가기 전에, 전화할게. Before I go there, I will call you.

긍정문 I will

☞ 오른쪽 힌트를 이용해서, 직접 문장을 만들어보세요!

훈련용 MP3

정답확인 : P 260

01	그 애가 좋아할 걸.	
02	너 Jennifer 만나봐야 돼. 너네 잘 맞을 걸.	잘 맞다, 친해지다 get along
03	너 시간 충분히 있을 거야. 걱정 안 해도 돼.	충분한 시간 enough time
04	그 애한테 물어봐도 돼. 그 애가 도와줄 걸.	
05	너 이거 필요할 거야. 가져가도 돼.	
06	걔네들 금방 도착할 거야.	
07	이거 입어 봐. 너한테 잘 어울릴 걸.	입어 봐 Try it on. 잘어울리다 look good on 사람
08	그거 쉬울 거야.	동사 자리에 동사가 없으면??!!
09	그거 똑같을 걸.	똑같은 the same/identical
10	그 애 바쁠 거야. 우리 그 애 귀찮게 안 하는 게 좋겠다.	귀찮게 하다 bother

긍정문 It will

☞ 오른쪽 힌트를 이용해서, 직접 문장을 만들어보세요!

11	그거 (아마) 쌀 거야.	
12	그거 그때 쯤이면 다 될 거야.	다 된, 준비 된 ready, 그때 쯤 by then
13	이따 비 올 걸.	
14	이거 오래 걸릴 거야.	
15	이거 돈 많이 들 거야.	
16	그거 될 거야. 난 확신해.	
17	그거 또 고장날 거야.	고장나다 break down
18	모든 게 괜찮을 거야.	
19	그게 문제일 거야.	문제 a problem
20	그거 곧 사라질 거야.	사라지다 disappear

부정문 I won't

☞ 오른쪽 힌트를 이용해서, 직접 문장을 만들어보세요!

21	그 애 그거 안 좋아할 거야. 🔊	
22	너 그거 필요 없을 걸. 🔊	
23	쉽지 않을 걸. 🔊	
24	그게 도움이 안 될 걸. 🔊	도움 되다 help/ 도움 되는 helpful
25	눈 안 올 거야. 🔊	
26	오래 안 걸릴 걸. 🔊	
27	돈 별로 안 들 거야. 🔊	별로 much
28	아프지 않을 거야. 🔊	
29	그거 안 될 걸. 🔊	
30	이런 일 다시는 없을 거야. 사과해. 🔊	일이 생기다, 일어나다 happen

의문문 Will?

☞ 오른쪽 힌트를 이용해서, 직접 문장을 만들어보세요!

31	다섯 시에 집에 있을 거야? 🔊	
32	몇 시에 돌아올 거야? 🔊	
33	비가 올까? 🔊	
34	이게 될까? 넌 어떻게 생각해? 🔊	
35	오래 걸릴까? 얼마나 오래 걸릴까? 나 시간 없는데. 🔊	
36	이게 또 바뀔까? 그거 자주 바뀌어. 🔊	
37	그게 나한테 잘 어울릴까? 그랬으면 좋겠다. 🔊	그랬으면 좋겠다. I hope so!
38	그런 일이 또 생길까? 안 그랬으면 좋겠다. 🔊	안 그랬으면 좋겠다. I hope not.
39	너 괜찮겠어? 나 너 걱정돼. 🔊	괜찮은 ok
40	5시 괜찮을까? 🔊	5시 = 주인공!

긍정문 I think I'll

☞ 오른쪽 힌트를 이용해서, 직접 문장을 만들어보세요!

41	난 오늘 밤에 집에 있을 것 같아. 아무 때나 전화해도 돼. 🔊	
42	그 애들 곧 결혼할 것 같아. 🔊	결혼하다 get married
43	Jim이 도와줄 것 같아. 그 앤 항상 'yes'라고 말해. 🔊	
44	모든 게 잘 될 것 같아. 🔊	잘되다, 잘풀리다 work out (well)
45	너 성공할 것 같아. 난 널 믿어! 🔊	성공하다 succeed, 믿다 believe in
46	두 시간 정도 걸릴 것 같아요. 🔊	
47	20불 들 것 같아. 지금 계산하실래요? 🔊	
48	그거 고치는데 비쌀 것 같아. 🔊	
49	이게 더 나을 것 같아. 🔊	더 나은 better
50	쉬워질 것 같아. 🔊	(더)쉬워지다 get easier

부정문 I don't think I'll

☞ 오른쪽 힌트를 이용해서, 직접 문장을 만들어보세요!

51	Paul은 안 올 것 같아.	
52	난 안 갈 것 같아.	
53	내일 테니스 안 칠 것 같아. 몸이 안 좋아.	몸이 좋은, 잘 있는 well
54	넌 문제 없을 것 같아.	없다=가지고 있지 않다
55	그 애 그거 없을 것 같아.	
56	이거 멈추지 않을 것 같아.	멈추다 stop
57	너가 후회할 것 같지 않아. 그냥 해!	
58	그 애 그거 잊어버리지 않을 것 같아.	
59	나아질 것 같지 않아.	나아지다 get better
60	더 나빠질 것 같지 않아.	(더) 나빠지다 get worse

의문문 Do you think you'll?

☞ 오른쪽 힌트를 이용해서, 직접 문장을 만들어보세요!

61	넌 언제 도착할 것 같아? 🔊	
62	그 애가 뭐라고 할 것 같아? 🔊	뭐라고 하다?? 행동하다의 하다? Or 말하다?
63	전 뭐가 필요할 것 같아요? 🔊	
64	넌 뭘 할 것 같아? 🔊	
65	넌 어디 갈 것 같아? 🔊	
66	그게 (사이즈가) 맞을 것 같아? 🔊	
67	그게 (무게가) 얼마 나갈 거 같아? 🔊	무게가 나가다 weigh
68	넌 거기서 얼마나 오래 있을 것 같아? 🔊	
69	우리 쇼핑 갈 시간 있을 것 같아? 🔊	쇼핑 가다 go shopping
70	넌 내가 포기할 것 같아? 난 그렇게 생각하지 않아. 🔊	난 그렇게 생각하지 않아. I don't think so.

의문문 Do you think you'll?

☞ 오른쪽 힌트를 이용해서, 직접 문장을 만들어보세요!

71	넌 내가 잘 할 것 같아? 왜 그렇게 생각해?	그렇게 so
72	얼마나 오래 걸릴 것 같아요?	
73	얼마 들 것 같아요? 대략?	대략? Roughly?
74	그게 가능할 것 같니?	
75	그게 문제일 것 같니?	
76	그게 언제일 것 같아요?	
77	이게 언제 다 될 것 같아요?	다 된, 준비된 ready
78	그게 좋은 생각일 것 같아?	좋은 생각 a good idea
79	그게 얼마일 것 같아요?	
80	이거면 충분할 것 같아?	충분한 enough

81	내가 Jenny 보면, 그 애한테 말할게.	
82	너 올 때까지, 내가 여기서 기다릴게.	
83	나 집에가면, 너한테 전화할게.	
84	그 애 오면, 내가 너한테 알려줄게.	
85	내가 나가기 전에, 문자할게.	
86	이거 다하고 나서, 그거 치울게.	
87	내가 집에 가자마자, 이메일 보낼게요.	
88	너가 그 애한테 물어보면, 그 애가 도와줄 걸.	
89	그 애 오는대로, 내가 그 애한테 말할게.	
90	내가 일 끝나기 전에, 이거 처리할게.	처리하다 take care of/handle

91	나 집에 가면, 바로 잘 거야. 🔊	바로 자다 go straight to bed
92	내가 돌아올 때, 선물 사올게. 약속해. 🔊	
93	너가 결정할 때까지, 기다릴게. 🔊	
94	도움이 필요하면, 알려줄래요? 돕고 싶어요. 🔊	
95	너 그거 하면, 후회할 거야. 안 하는 게 좋을 것 같아. 🔊	
96	내가 그거 하기 전에, 다시 확인할게. 🔊	
97	집에 도착하자마자, 문자해줄래? 🔊	
98	너 그 애 보면, 그 애한테 말 좀 해줄래? 🔊	
99	이거 다 한 후에, 날 불러줄래? 🔊	call 부르다
100	너 준비되면, 메시지 남겨줄래? 🔊	메시지 남기다 leave a message

복습강의 MP3

Positive (긍정)		Negative (부정)		Question (의문)	
I am -ing	해, 하고있어 (지금)	I'm not -ing	안 해, 안 하고 있어	Are you -ing?	해? (지금) 하고 있어?
I 동사	해 (원래)	I don't	안 해	Do you?	해? (원래)
I will	할걸, 할거야 (예측)	I won't	안 할 걸, 안 할 거야	Will you?	할까? 할꺼야? (예측)
I think I'll	할 것 같아	I don't think I'll	안 할 것 같아	Do you think you'll	할 것 같아?

01	영어 공부하고싶어.	17	그 앤 공부를 열심히 안 해. 공부에 관심이 없어. [관심있는 into/interested in]
02	너가 원하면, 거기서 공부해도 돼.	18	난 일요일엔 영어 공부 안 해.
03	여기서 공부하기 힘들어. 집중이 안 돼. (=못 해)	19	너가 원하지 않으면, 공부 하지 않아도 돼.
04	올해는 영어공부를 열심히 하는 게 좋을 것 같아.	20	나 내일 공부할 시간이 있을까? 없을 것 같아.
05	집에 가면, 영어 공부할 거야.	21	뭐 공부하고 싶어?
06	내일 너랑 공부할 수 있어.	22	뭐 공부할 거야?
07	그 직업을 원하면, 공부 열심히 해야 돼.	23	영어 공부해야 되나?
08	난 매일 한 시간씩 영어 공부해.	24	우리 같이 공부할까? 재미있을 거야.
09	나 지금 공부하는데. 그거 내가 나중에 해도 될까?	25	너 매일 영어 공부해? 언제 공부해?
10	그 앤 공부 정말 열심히 해.	26	공부할 시간 있어?
11	영어 공부하는 거 재미있어!	27	전 이 분야에 관심이 있는데요, 제가 뭘 공부하는 게 좋을 것 같아요? [이 분야 this field]
12	같이 공부하면 재미있을 것 같아요.	28	지금 공부하니? 뭐 공부해?
13	나 지금은 공부 안 할래. 나중에 할게.	29	거기서 공부해도 돼?
14	나 지금 공부하는 거 아니었어. 괜찮아. 우리 지금 통화할 수 있어.	30	너가 크면, 넌 뭘 공부할 것 같아? [너가 크면(=커서) when you grow up]
15	여기서 공부 못 하겠어. 너무 시끄럽다. [시끄러운 loud]		
16	난 그 애랑 공부 안 할거야. 혼자 할거야.		

정답확인 : P 263

A: Do you have/provide dry cleaning services?

B: Yes, we have/offer/provide dry cleaning services. Do you want to use it? / Would you like to use them?

A: Yes, please. I think I will need it tonight. How can I use the service?

B: You can dial 4 from your phone in your room. Or you can bring it to me.

A: Thank you for your help.

B: Any time.

—

A: I'd like to use the dry cleaning service(, please). / I want to use the dry cleaning service.

B: Yes/Sure. What is your room number?

A: It is 405.

B: I will pick it up now.

A: When do you think I will have it back? Will it take long?

B: It usually takes a day. So, you can have it back tomorrow.

A: I have to wear it tonight. Will it be possible to have/get it back tonight?

B: Yes, it is possible. But, it will cost 10 dollars extra/more./ It will cost extra 10 dollars.

A: When do I have to pay for this? Can I pay when I check out?

B: Yes. You can pay when you check out.

—

A: Do you have a laundry room here?

B: Yes, we do. / Yes, we have it. We have 4 washing machines and dryers.

A: That's good. Where is the laundry room?

B: It is on the first floor.

호텔 드라이 클리닝 서비스

A: 드라이 클리닝 서비스를 제공하나요? [제공하다 provide / 있다, 가지고 있다 have]

B: 네, 저희 드라이클리닝 서비스 있어요. 사용하실래요?

A: 네, 오늘밤에 필요할 것 같은데요. 제가 어떻게 그 서비스를 이용할 수 있지요?

B: 당신의 방 전화로 4번을 걸어도[걸다 dial] 되고요. 제게 가져다 주셔도 돼요.

A: 도와주셔서 감사해요.

B: 언제든지요. [Any time!]

—

A: 드라이 클리닝 서비스를 이용하고 싶어요.

B: 네. 당신의 방 넘버가 뭐예요?

A: 405예요.

B: 지금 가지러 갈게요.

A: 언제 제가 다시 받을 수 있을 것 같아요?[다시 받다 have-back] 오래 걸릴까요?

B: 보통 하루 걸려요. 그래서 내일 받을 수 있어요.

A: 오늘 밤에 입어야 하는데요. 오늘밤에 다시 받는 게 가능할
   까요?

B: 네, 가능해요. 하지만, 10불 더 들거예요.

A: 언제 이거 계산해야 되죠? 체크아웃할 때 계산해도 되나
   요?

B: 네, 체크아웃할 때, 계산하셔도 돼요.

—

A: 여기에 세탁실[a laundry room] 있나요?

B: 네, 있어요. 세탁기와 건조기 네 대가 있어요.

A: 좋네요. 세탁실이 어디있죠?

B: 1층에 있어요.

세탁실

A: Can I use the washing machine and the dryer?

B: Yes, you can use them. You have to have some coins.

A: How much does it cost to use the washing machine?

B: It costs 2 dollars.

A: How about the dryer?

B: It costs 2 dollars. But I think you will need more than 2 dollars to use the dryer.

A: How much do you think I will need to use the washing machine and the dryer?

B: I think you will need 6 dollars.

A: I don't have (any) change. Can you change this 10 dollar bill/note?

B: Sure. / Of course.

A: I want to do the/some laundry. Do you have a washing machine and a dryer?

B: Yes, we do. / Yes we have them. I will show you the laundry room.

A: How do I/you use this washing machine?

B: You put (your/the) coins here. You put washing powder/detergent here. And you press/push this button.

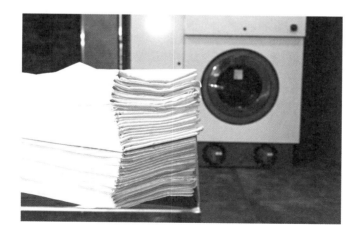

세탁실

A: 세탁기랑 건조기를 사용해도 되나요?

B: 네, 그것들 사용해도 됩니다. 동전을 좀 가지고 있어야 해요.

A: 세탁기 사용하는데 돈이 얼마 드나요?

B: 2불 들어요.

A: 건조기는요?

B: 2불 드는데요, 건조기를 사용하는데는 2불보다 더 필요할 것 같아요.

A: 세탁기랑 건조기를 사용하는데 제가 얼마 필요할 것 같아요?

B: 6불 필요할 거 같아요.

A: 잔돈이 없는데요. 이 10불을 바꿔줄 수 있어요?

B: 물론이죠.

A: 빨래를 하고 싶은데요. [빨래하다 do the laundry] 세탁기랑 건

조기 있나요?

B: 네, 있어요. 제가 세탁실 보여줄게요.

A: 이 세탁기 어떻게 사용하죠? [언제??-원래!!]

B: 여기에 동전을 넣고요. 여기에 세제[washing powder/detergent]

를 넣어요. 그리고 이 버튼을 눌러요.

Unit

4

추측을 말하고 싶을 때

추측을 말하고 싶을 때

may & might '~할지도 몰라, 할 수도 있어'

May나 **might**는 아직 불확실 하거나, 어떤 사람 또는 상황에 대해 추측 할 때 아주 유용하게 쓰이는 표현이에요. May를 사용할 때가 might를 사용할 때보다 확신이나 가능성이 조금 더 높아요.

하지만, 의문문에서 **"May I?"**는 추측을 나타내지 않고, 허락을 요청하는 정중 한 표현입니다.

Positive (긍정)	Negative (부정)	Question (의문)
I may/might	I may not / might not	May I?
~할지도 몰라 ~할 수도 있어	~ 안 할지도 몰라 ~ 안 할 수도 있어	~해도 되나요? [허락을 요청하는 정중한 표현]

해설강의 MP3

이렇게 만듭니다!

문장의 핵심단어인 '동사'를 넣습니다!

Positive (긍정)	Negative (부정)	Question (의문)
나 거기 갈지도 몰라. I may / might go there.	난 안 갈지도 몰라. I may / might not go.	저 지금 가도 되나요? May I go now?

<심화표현>

Might as well ~하지 뭐, 그러지 뭐!

'지금 상황을 보니, 그냥 그렇게 하는 게 좋겠다'는 의미로 활용도가 높은 표현이에요!

예: 그럼 여기서 기다리지 뭐.

I might as well wait here.

정답확인 : P 264

01	우리 이따가 쇼핑 갈 수도 있어.	쇼핑 가다 go shopping
02	너 그거 금방 받을 수도 있어.	받다 get/receive
03	너 속이 안 좋을 수도 있어.	속이 안 좋다 feel sick
04	너 후회할지도 몰라.	후회하다 regret
05	나 오늘 일 늦게 끝날지도 몰라.	
06	너가 웃을지도 몰라. 하지만, 난 심각해.	
07	우리 운이 좋을 수도 있어. 누가 알아?	누가 알아? Who knows?
08	너가 맞을지도 몰라.	맞는, 옳은 right
09	내가 틀릴 수도 있어.	틀린, 잘못 된 wrong
10	그 애 아플지도 몰라.	

11	나 다음주에 태국에 갈지도 몰라. 내 친구 중 한 명이 거기 살아. 🔊	내 친구 중 한 명 a friend of mine
12	우리 내일 늦게 올 수도 있어. 우리 없어 시작해도 돼. 🔊	
13	Danny가 이거 좋아할지도 몰라. 🔊	
14	우리 이거 나중에 필요할지도 몰라. 그냥 가지고 있을 거야. 🔊	
15	우리 이번 주말에 수영장에 갈지도 몰라. 너도 올래? 🔊	
16	Tim도 올 수도 있어.	
17	Simon이 일찍 올지도 몰라. 그 앤 항상 일찍 와. 🔊	
18	너 그거 잃어버릴지도 몰라. 집에 두고 가는 게 나아. 🔊	두고 가다 leave
19	나 그거 까먹을지도 몰라. 나한테 이따 다시 말해줄래? 🔊	
20	나 지금 못 나가. 중요한 전화를 기다리고 있어. 그 애가 금방 전화할지도 몰라. 🔊	중요한 전화 an important call

긍정문 It may

☞ 오른쪽 힌트를 이용해서, 직접 문장을 만들어보세요!

21	오늘 오후에 비가 올지도 몰라. 🔊	오늘 오후 this afternoon
22	내일 눈이 많이 올지도 몰라. 🔊	
23	이거 금방 시작할지도 몰라. 🔊	
24	이거 금방 끝날 수도 있어. 🔊	
25	오래 걸릴 수도 있어. 🔊	
26	돈이 많이 들지도 몰라. 🔊	
27	그게 오늘 저녁에 올지도 몰라. 🔊	
28	너의 계획이 될지도 몰라. 해보는 게 좋을 것 같아. 🔊	
29	그거 또 바뀔지도 몰라. 🔊	
30	그거 또 고장날지도 몰라. 🔊	

긍정문 It might

☞ 오른쪽 힌트를 이용해서, 직접 문장을 만들어보세요!

31	위험할지도 몰라. 🔊	위험한 dangerous
32	너무 독할 수도 있어. 🔊	독한 strong
33	비어 있을지도 몰라. 🔊	빈 empty
34	가짜일지도 몰라. 🔊	가짜인, 짝퉁인 fake
35	이상할지도 몰라. 🔊	이상한 weird/strange
36	내 잘못일지도 몰라. 🔊	내 잘못 my fault
37	뭔가 잘못 됐는지도 몰라. 🔊	
38	비쌀지도 몰라. 🔊	
39	그게 가능할지도 몰라. 🔊	
40	어색할지도 몰라. 🔊	어색한,불편한 awkward

부정문 I may not

☞ 오른쪽 힌트를 이용해서, 직접 문장을 만들어보세요!

41	난 거기 안 갈지도 몰라. 솔직히, 가고 싶지 않아. 🔊	솔직히 to be honest/to be frank
42	**우린 거기 오래 안 있을지도 몰라.** 🔊	
43	그 애 그거 안 가져올지도 몰라. 🔊	
44	**우리 이사 안 갈지도 몰라.** 🔊	
45	그 애가 그거 안 좋아할지도 몰라. 🔊	
46	**그 애가 동의하지 않을지도 몰라.** 🔊	동의하다 agree
47	걔네들은 배달 안 할지도 몰라. 🔊	
48	**걔네들은 일요일에 문 안 열지도(영업 안 할지도) 몰라.** 🔊	
49	짐은 가고 싶어 하지 않을 수도 있어. 🔊	
50	**그 애가 널 보고 싶어 하지 않을 수도 있어.** 🔊	

51	큰 일이 아닐지도 몰라. 확실히 알기 전까진, 걱정하지 않는 게 좋겠어. 🔊	큰 일 a big deal, 확실히 알다 know for sure
52	거기 없을지도 몰라. 🔊	
53	아직 안 됐을지도 몰라. 🔊	(다) 된, 준비된 ready
54	그거 모자랄지도 몰라. 🔊	모자란=충분하지 않은
55	실수가 아닐지도 몰라. (그건) 고의 일지도 몰라. 🔊	고의 on purpose
56	심각하지 않을지도 몰라. 🔊	
57	이거 금방 안 끝날지도 몰라. 이거 보통 오래 걸려. 🔊	
58	비 안 올지도 몰라. 🔊	
59	그거 안 될 수도 있어. 🔊	
60	오래 안 걸리지도 몰라. 🔊	

의문문 May I?

☞ 오른쪽 힌트를 이용해서, 직접 문장을 만들어보세요!

61	저 지금 가도 되나요? 🔊	
62	저 들어가도 되나요? 🔊	들어가다 come in
63	저 오늘 일찍 (나)가도 되나요? 🔊	일찍 (나)가다 leave early
64	여기 앉아도 될까요? 🔊	
65	뭔가 물어봐도 되나요? 🔊	
66	제가 질문 하나 해도 될까요? 🔊	질문하다 ask a question
67	제가 개인적인 질문해도 될까요? 🔊	개인적인 질문 a personal question
68	이거 써도 되나요? 🔊	
69	화장실에 가도 되나요? 🔊	
70	화장실을 써도 되나요? 🔊	

의문문 May I?

☞ 오른쪽 힌트를 이용해서, 직접 문장을 만들어보세요!

71	제가 이거 해봐도 되나요? 🔊	
72	제가 먼저 해도 되나요? 🔊	먼저 하다 go first
73	제가 그거 봐도 되나요? 🔊	보다 see/look at/have a look/ take a look
74	왜(그런건지)인지 물어봐도 되나요? 🔊	왜인지 why
75	이 의자 가져가도 될까요? 🔊	
76	귀찮게 해서 죄송한데요, 이것 좀 빌려도 될까요? 🔊	귀찮게 하다, 방해하다 bother
77	중간에 말 끊어서 죄송한데요, 저 잠깐 밖에 나가도 괜찮을까요? 🔊	중간에 끼어들다, 말 끊다 interrupt
78	이 전화 받아도 될까요? 🔊	
79	제가 다시 해봐도 되나요? 🔊	
80	생각해봐도 되나요? 결정하면, 알려줄게요. 🔊	

긍정문 I might as well

☞ 오른쪽 힌트를 이용해서, 직접 문장을 만들어보세요!

81	그럼 오늘하지 뭐.	
82	지금 가지 뭐.	
83	이것도 사지 뭐.	
84	우리 조금 더 기다려보지 뭐.	조금 더 a bit longer
85	밖에 **비** 와. 여기 있지 뭐.	
86	그러지 뭐.	
87	저것도 갈지(교체하지) 뭐.	갈다, 교체하다 replace
88	이거 (선물) 포장하지 뭐.	선물 포장하다 gift wrap
89	벽하고 얘기하지 뭐.	벽 the wall
90	우리 그냥 다른 데 가지 뭐.	다른 데 somewhere else

91	내가 그걸 피할 수 없다면, 그냥 즐기지 뭐.	피하다 avoid
92	우리 이거 지금 그냥 다 하지 뭐.	
93	멀지 않아. 거기 걸어가지 뭐.	
94	우리 사실대로 말하지 뭐. 그 애 알 걸.	사실대로 말하다, 털어놓다 come clean
95	우리 여기서 잠깐 멈추지 뭐.	
96	지금 취소가 안 되면(못 한다면), 가죠 뭐.	
97	너한테 말하지 뭐. 모두 다 이미 아는데.	everybody = 단수취급!
98	둘 다 가져가지 뭐. 우리 둘 다 필요할지도 몰라.	둘 다 both
99	우리 지금 나가지 뭐.	
100	우리가 이 상황에서 빠져나갈 수 없다면, 이걸 최대한 활용해 보죠 뭐.	빠져나가다 get out of, 최대한 활용하다 make the most of

Positive (긍정)		Negative (부정)		Question (의문)	
I am -ing	해, 하고있어 (지금)	I'm not -ing	안 해, 안하고있어	Are you -ing?	해? (지금) 하고 있어?
I 동사	해 (원래)	I don't	안 해	Do you?	해? (원래)
I will	할 걸, 할 거야 (예측)	I won't	안 할 걸, 안 할 거야	Will you?	할까? 할꺼야? (예측)
I think I'll	할 것 같아	I don't think I'll	안 할 것 같아	Do you think you'll	할 것 같아?
I may I might	할지도 몰라, 할 수도 있어	I may not I might not	안할지도 몰라, 안할 수도 있어	May I?	해도 돼요? (허락)

01	너가 원하면, 나 여기 있을 수 있어.	17	그 애 오래 안 있을 걸.
02	우리 오늘은 여기 있어야 돼.	18	우리 거기 오래 있으면 안 돼.
03	너 올 때까지, 여기 있을게.	19	나 지금은 거기 안 있는데. 나 삼촌 집에 있어.
04	여기서 3일 밤 동안 머무르고 싶어요.	20	난 거기 오래 안 있어. 거기 좀 불편해.
05	나 거기 가면, 내 친구 집에 있을 거야. 내 친구가 거기 살아.	21	그 애 우리랑 안 있을지도 몰라. 그 앤 호텔을 더 좋아해.
06	너 여기 있어도 돼.	22	넌 어디 있을거야?
07	난 친구랑 있을지도 몰라. 아직 확실하지 않아.	23	우리 거기서 얼마나 있어야 돼?
08	나 집에 하루종일 있을 것 같아. 아무때나 오셔도 돼요.	24	우리가 어디서 있는 게 좋을 것 같아?
09	난 호텔에서 묵고 있어.	25	하룻밤 더 여기서 머무르는 게 가능한가요?
10	그 애 한국에 오면, 항상 우리랑 있어.	26	나 여기 잠깐만 있어도 될까? 너무 피곤해.
11	우리 그냥 여기서 있지 뭐.	27	우리집에서 있을래? 너가 원하면, 그래도 돼.
12	너 우리집에 있는 게 좋겠어.	28	넌 일본 가면, 어디서 머물러? 가족이 거기 있니?
13	난 여기서 있기 싫어.	29	어디서 머무르고 있어요?
14	난 여기 더 이상 못 있겠어.	30	얼마나 오래 거기 있을 수 있어?
15	우리 여기 안 있어도 돼. 우리 다른데로 가도 돼.	31	여기서 잠깐만 있어줄래? 금방 돌아올게.
16	난 거기 안 있을 것 같아.	32	넌 어디서 머무를 것 같아? 결정하면, 알려줄래?

정답확인 : P 267

감기 등의 증상

A: You look sick. Are you ok?

B: I am not well. / I am not feeling well. / I don't feel well. I am feeling sick, too. I might have a cold.

A: I think you should see a doctor. I will take you there.

B: Thanks. My body is aching all over.

A: If you just sit here, I will get/bring my car. And, what do you need?

B: I need my purse/wallet. It is in my room. It will be on the desk. / It is going to be on the desk.

—

A: Excuse me, where is the nearest clinic from here?

B: It is on Helly Road.

A: How can I go/get there?

B: You can walk there. / You can go there on foot. It is two blocks away from here.

A: You don't look well. You look tired, too. Do you have a cold?

B: No, I don't have a cold. But I have a headache.

A: I think you should take this medicine.

B: What is it?

A: It is a painkiller.

B: I might as well take it now.

A: I hope you get better soon.

—

A: How is your headache? Is it getting better?

B: It is getting better. Thank you for asking.

A: 너 아파 보여. 괜찮아?

B: 나 몸이 좀 안 좋아. 지금 속도 안 좋아.[속이 안 좋다, 울렁이다 feel sick] 감기 걸린지도 몰라. [감기 걸리다 have a cold]

A: 병원에 가보는 게 좋을 것 같아. [병원에 가다 see a doctor] 내가 거기 데려다 줄게.

B: 고마워. 온몸이 다 아파. [아프다 ache, 여기저기 다 all over]

A: 너 그냥 여기 앉아있으면, 내가 차 가져올게. 그리고, 너 뭐 필요해?

B: 내 지갑 필요해. 내 방에 있어. 책상 위에 있을거야.

—

A: 실례지만, 여기서 가장 가까운 클리닉이 어디있어요?

B: Helly Road에 있어요.

A: 거기에 어떻게 갈 수 있어요?

B: 걸어 갈 수 있어요. 여기서 두 블록 떨어져 있어요.

A: 너 안 좋아 보여. 피곤해 보이기도 하고. 감기 걸렸니?

B: 아니 감기 안 걸렸어. 근데, 머리가 아파. [머리 아프다, 두통 있다 have a headache]

A: 너 이 약 먹는 게 좋을 것 같아. [약 먹다 take medicine]

B: 뭔데?

A: 진통제야. [진통제 a painkiller]

B: 지금 먹지 뭐.

A: 빨리 낫길 바라. [I hope you get better soon.]

—

A: 너 머리 아픈 것은 어때? 좀 나아지고 있어?

B: 나아지고 있어. 물어봐줘서 고마워. [Thank you for -ing]

Dialogue Practice

감기 등의 증상

A: I have a terrible headache. Do you have a painkiller?

B: Here it is. / Here you are. I think you should take one now.

A: I will (do that/take it) . Thank you. How much is it?

B: It is 10 dollars.

A: How many (pills) do I take?

B: If it is terrible/bad, you can take two.

—

A: How can I help (you)?

B: I have the flu.

A: Do you have a fever, too?

B: Yes (, I do). I have a fever. I have a sore throat. And I have a runny nose.

A: I will prescribe some medicine (for you). I will prescribe (some) antibiotics, too.

B: Thanks.

기초영어 1000문장 말하기 연습 2

A: You have to drink a lot of/plenty of water. You have to rest.

B: I will try. Where is the/a pharmacy/chemist? Where do I have to go?

A: It is downstairs. It is next to the bookstore. It is easy to find.

감기 등의 증상

A: 머리 엄청[terrible] 아파요. 진통제 있어요?

B: 여기요. 지금 하나 드시는 게 좋겠어요.

A: 그럴게요. 고마워요. 얼마예요?

B: 10불이에요.

A: 몇 개 먹나요?

B: 많이 나쁘면(아프면), 2개 드셔도 돼요.

—

A: 제가 어떻게 도와드릴 수 있을까요?

B: 독감 걸렸어요. [독감 걸리다 have the flu]

A: 열도 있나요? [have a fever]

B: 네, 열도 나고요. 목이 아파요. [have a sore throat] 콧물 나요.

[have a runny nose]

A: 약좀 처방해드릴게요. [처방하다 prescribe] 항생제[antibiotics]도

처방해 드릴게요.

B: 고마워요.

A: 물 많이 드셔야 하고요. 쉬셔야 돼요.

B: 노력할게요. 약국은 어디에요? 어디로 가야돼요?

A: 아래층에 있어요. 서점 옆에[next to] 있어요 찾기 쉬워요

Unit

5

'과거'에 한 일을 말하고 싶을 때

Unit 5

'과거'에 한 일을 말하고 싶을 때

동사 과거형 '~했어, 했었어'

과거에 이미 **한 일**에 대해서 말할 때 과거시제를 사용해요. 한국어는 주로 쌍시옷 받침을 사용해서 과거를 표현하는 것처럼 (먹었어, 갔었어), 영어의 '과거'는 주로 동사 뒤에 **–ed**를 붙여서 만들어요. (불규칙 동사는 Unit 0 참고)

Positive (긍정)	Negative (부정)	Question (의문)
I 과거형 (stayed/went)	I didn't	Did **you?**
~했어, ~했었어	~안 했어	~했어?

부정문에서는 현재형 don't의 과거형인 **didn't**를 사용하고, 의문문에서는 Do you?가 과거의 형태인 **Did** you?로 **이미 변환된** 것이어서, 뒤에 따라오는 동사는 편하게 원형을 사용하면 돼요!

이렇게 만듭니다!

- 문장의 핵심단어인 '동사'를 넣습니다!

- 긍정문에서는 과거동사를 사용하고, 부정문과 의문문에서는 didn't/did가 이미 과거형이기 때문에 동사원형을 넣어요!

Positive (긍정)	Negative (부정)	Question (의문)
난 그거 좋았어. I liked it.	난 그거 별로 였어. I didn't like it.	넌 그거 좋았어? Did you like it?
나 거기 갔었어. I went there.	난 거기 안 갔어. I didn't go there.	너 거기 갔었어? Did you go there?

<함께 쓰는 단어>

과거의 시간을 나타내는 단어: yesterday, last, ago, when

<스펠링 법칙>

1. e로 끝나는 단어는 뒤에 그냥 d만 붙여요! [예: liked, changed]
2. -y 로 끝나는 단어
① 모음(a,e,i,o,u) + y : 는 그냥 -ed 붙입니다 [예: stayed]
② 자음 + y : y 떼고 -ied [예: studied, tried, cried]

긍정문 I 과거

☞ 오른쪽 힌트를 이용해서, 직접 문장을 만들어보세요!

훈련용 MP3

정답확인 : P 267

01	**나 10분 전에 왔어.**	오다 come-came-come, 10분 전 10 minutes ago
02	**내가 그거 했어.**	하다 do-did-done
03	**나 이거 어제 샀어.**	사다 buy-bought-bought
04	**나 어젯밤에 잠 잘 잤어.**	자다 sleep-slept-slept
05	**오늘 아침에 손가락을 베었어.**	베다, 자르다 cut-cut-cut
06	**어제 손을 데었어.**	데다, 타다 burn
07	**오늘 아침에 늦게 일어났어.**	get-got-got
08	**이거 널 위해서 만든 거야.**	make-made-made
09	**며칠 전에 Sam 만났어.**	만나다 meet-met-met, 며칠 전 a few days ago/the other day
10	**우리 점심 같이 먹었어.**	먹다 eat-ate-eaten

11	나 그거 찾았어. 🔊	찾다 find-found-found
12	이미 알고 있었어. 🔊	알다 know-knew-known
13	거기에 친구랑 갔었어. 🔊	가다 go-went-gone
14	내 반지 잃어버렸어. 너무 속상해. 🔊	잃어버리다 lose-lost-lost
15	그 애 5시에 나갔어. 🔊	나가다 leave-left-left
16	나 지갑을 집에 두고왔어. 🔊	두고가다/두고오다 leave-left-left
17	너 잘 했어! 난 네가 자랑스러워! 🔊	하다 do-did-done, 자랑스러운 proud of
18	깜빡 했다. 미안. 🔊	깜빡하다, 잊다 forget-forgot-forgotten
19	너한테 전화한다는 걸 깜빡했어. 🔊	동사를 두개 넣고 싶으면??
20	너한테 말해준다는 걸 깜빡했어. 🔊	

21	저 영수증 가져왔어요.	가져오다 bring-brouht-brought
22	그 애가 그거 가져갔어.	가져가다 take-took-taken
23	너 그거 벌써 말했어. 그래서 **알아**.	말하다 say-said-said
24	그 애가 나한테 말해줬어. 그래서 알고있었어.	말해주다 tell-told-told
25	좋은 시간 보냈어요. 고마워요.	좋은 시간 보내다 have a good time, have-had-had
26	그거 아팠어.	아프다 hurt-hurt-hurt
27	오래 걸렸어.	걸리다 take-took-taken
28	거기 가는데 오래 걸렸어.	
29	돈 많이 들었어.	돈이 들다 cost-cost-cost
30	그거 설치하는데 돈 많이 들었어.	

긍정문 I 과거

☞ 오른쪽 힌트를 이용해서, 직접 문장을 만들어보세요!

31	나 어제 하루종일 일했어. 🔊	하루종일 all day
32	TV 봤어. 🔊	
33	너 일찍 도착했네. 🔊	
34	우리 거기에서 일주일 있었어. 🔊	
35	그거 막 시작했어. 🔊	막 just
36	그거 1시간 전에 끝났어. 🔊	
37	그거 됐어! 🔊	
38	어제 하루종일 비 왔어. 🔊	
39	그거 갑자기 멈췄어. 🔊	갑자기 suddenly
40	그거 달라 보였어. 🔊	보이다 look

41	너한테 뭔가 **물어보고 싶었어.** 〰	하고 싶었어 = 하고 싶어의 과거!
42	**나 거기에 가고 싶었는데.** 〰	
43	나 그거 사고 싶었어. 〰	
44	**나 그거 갖고 싶었는데. 고마워.** 〰	
45	결정했어. 〰	
46	**우리 거기 같이 가기로 했어.** 〰	하기로 하다 = 결정하다!
47	나 그거 **하기로 했어.** 〰	
48	**아무것도 안 바꾸기로 했어.** 〰	안 하기로 하다 = decide not to
49	포기 안 하기로 했어. 〰	
50	**그거 안 하기로 했어.** 〰	

51	나 아무 말도 안 했어.	
	🔊	
52	나 아무한테도 말 안 했어.	
	🔊	
53	걔네 안 왔어.	
	🔊	
54	나 그거 안 했어.	
	🔊	
55	나 아무것도 안 샀어. 신용카드가 없었거든.	없었다 = 가지고 있지 않았다
	🔊	
56	시간이 없었어.	
	🔊	
57	아무것도 할 시간이 없었어.	
	🔊	
58	거기 갈 시간이 없었어.	
	🔊	
59	전화할 시간이 없었어.	
	🔊	
60	나 그거 거기다 두지 않았는데. 이상하네.	
	🔊	

부정문 I didn't
☞ 오른쪽 힌트를 이용해서, 직접 문장을 만들어보세요!

61	나 어제 Jim 봤는데, 아는 척 안 하더라. 🔊	아는 척하다 say hello
62	그거 생각 안 해봤어. 🔊	
63	몰랐어요. 🔊	
64	나 아무것도 안 했어. 🔊	
65	나 그거 진심이 아니었어. 미안해. 🔊	진심이다, 뜻하다 mean
66	어제 비 안 왔어. 🔊	
67	오래 안 걸렸어. 🔊	
68	그거 안 깨졌어. 🔊	
69	아무 말도 하고 싶지 않았어. 그래서 안 했어. 🔊	
70	아무 데도 가고 싶지 않았어. 그래서 안 갔지. 🔊	

71	어제 뭐 했어? 🔊	
72	뭐라고? (=뭐라고 했어?) 못 들었어. 🔊	
73	왜 전화했어? 🔊	
74	왜 그랬어? 🔊	
75	넌 뭐 봤어? 🔊	
76	어디 갔었어? 🔊	
77	얼마 주고 샀어? (=얼마 냈어?) 🔊	
78	어제 Simon 만났어? 어디 갔었니? 🔊	
79	좋은 시간 보냈어? 🔊	좋은 시간 보내다 have a good time
80	좋은 주말 보냈어? 🔊	좋은 주말 보내다 have a good weekend

81	언제 왔어? 🔊	
82	오래 기다렸어? 늦어서 미안. 🔊	
83	잘 잤어? 🔊	
84	점심 먹었어? 뭐 먹었어? 🔊	
85	언제 돌아왔어? 🔊	
86	거기 얼마나 오래 있었어? 🔊	
87	뭐 샀어? 🔊	
88	이거 어디서 샀어? 🔊	
89	영수증 가져왔어요? 🔊	
90	이거 어디서 났어? 🔊	나다, 찾다, 구하다 get

의문문 Did you?

☞ 오른쪽 힌트를 이용해서, 직접 문장을 만들어보세요!

91	뭔가 잃어버렸니? 뭔가 찾아?	
92	어디다 뒀는데?	
93	너 그 소식 들었니?	듣다 hear
94	어떡하다 그랬어? (=이거 어떻게 한거야?)	
95	왜 망설였어?	망설이다 hesitate
96	이해했어?	이해하다 understand/get
97	비 왔어?	
98	오래 걸렸니? 얼마나 오래 걸렸어?	
99	왜 이렇게 오래 걸렸어?	
100	그거 얼마 들었어?	

복습강의 MP3

Positive (긍정)		Negative (부정)		Question (의문)	
I am -ing	해, 하고있어 (지금)	I'm not -ing	안 해, 안하고있어	Are you -ing?	해? (지금) 하고 있어?
I 동사	해 (원래)	I don't	안 해	Do you?	해? (원래)
I will	할 걸, 할 거야 (예측)	I won't	안 할 걸, 안 할 거야	Will you?	할까? 할꺼야? (예측)
I think I'll	할 것 같아	I don't think I'll	안 할 것 같아	Do you think you'll	할 것 같아?
I may I might	할지도 몰라, 할 수도 있어	I may not I might not	안할지도 몰라, 안할 수도 있어	May I?	해도 돼요? (허락)
I 과거	했어, 했었어	I didn't	안 했어	Did you?	했어?

01	너가 괜찮다면, 여기서 기다릴래.	17	그게 우릴 기다려줄 것 같지 않아.
02	나 올 때까지, 너 여기서 기다려야 돼.	18	저 아무도 기다리고 있지 않아요. 여기 혼자예요.
03	기다릴 수 있어요. 괜찮아요.	19	그 앤 (원래) 아무도 기다리지 않아.
04	**10분 더 기다릴거야.** [10분 더 10 more minutes]	20	오래 기다리지 않았어. 나 여기 방금 왔어.
05	우리 기다려 보는 게 좋을 것 같아.	21	여기서 잠깐만 기다려줄래요?
06	여기서 기다리셔도 돼요.	22	얼마나 오래 기다려야 되나요? 오래 걸릴까요?
07	여기서 널 기다릴게.	23	여기서 기다려도 되나요?
08	친구 기다리고 있어서요. 이따가 주문해도 될까요?	24	우리가 기다리는 게 좋을 것 같아?
09	우리 여기서 기다리지 뭐.	25	어디서 기다릴거야?
10	그 앤 항상 늦어. 난 항상 그 앨 기다리고.	26	그 애가 우릴 기다릴 것 같아?
11	그 애가 **기다리고 있을지도** 몰라.	27	뭘 기다리고 있어? 그냥 해!
12	나 너 기다렸는데.	28	우리 어디서 기다릴까?
13	기다리는 거 쉽지 않아. 별로야(=난 그게 좋지 않아).	29	누군가 기다리고 있어요? 아님 지금 주문하실래요?
14	더 이상은 못 기다리겠어. 난 갈거야.	30	오래 기다렸어? 얼마나 오래 기다렸니?
15	오래 기다리지 않아도 돼요.	31	너 도착하면, 나 기다려줄래? 5분이면 도착할 것 같아.
16	기다리고 싶지 않아. 지금 시작하고 싶어.	32	그거 보통 얼마나 오래 기다려? 오래 걸려?

정답확인 : P 270

식당

A: I want to(=I'd like to) reserve a table for 4 people.

B: Sure.

A: Will it be possible to reserve a table for/at 7?

B: When will that reservation be? Is it (for) tonight/this evening?

A: Yes, it is (for) this evening.

B: Can I have your name, please?

A: My name is Yuna Jung.

B: How do you spell that/your name?

A: It is Y-U-N-A J-U-N-G.

B: Ok. I will see you at 7.

—

A: Do you have a reservation? / Did you make a reservation?

B: Yes, I have a reservation. / I made a reservation. My name is Yuna Jung. Is this our table?

A: Yes, it is. / Yes, that's right.

A: I don't have a reservation. / I didn't make a reservation.

But do you have a table for two?

B: Yes. Can you follow me?

A: Can we sit there?

B: I'm afraid, that table is reserved.

You can have/take this table.

A: Yes. This table is good, too.

식당

A: 네 명을 위한 테이블을 예약하고 싶어요.

B: 물론이죠.

A: 7시로 테이블 예약 가능할까요?

B: 그 예약이 언제일까요? 오늘 저녁인가요?

A: 네, 오늘 저녁이요.

B: 성함 (알려)주세요.

A: 제 이름은 유나 정이에요.

B: 스펠링이 어떻게 되죠? (=어떻게 너의 이름을 스펠해요? [원래!])

A: Y-u-n-a J-u-n-g이에요.

B: 알겠어요. 7시에 뵐게요.

—

A: 예약하셨나요? (=예약 가지고 있나요?)

B: 네, 예약했어요. 제 이름은 유나 정이에요.

이게 저희 테이블인가요?

A: 네, 맞아요.

A: 저 예약은 안 했는데요. 두 명을 위한 테이블 있나요?

B: 네, 따라와주실래요?

A: 저기 앉아도 되나요?

B: 유감이지만, 저 테이블은 예약 되었어요. [예약 된 reserved]이

테이블로 하셔도(have) 돼요.

A: 네, 이 테이블도 좋네요.

식당

A: Do you think it will be possible to reserve a table for tonight now?

B: Hang on. Let me check. / I will check.

A: For how many people?

B: For two people.

A: I'm afraid (that), we are fully booked.

A: Can I ask something? / May I ask something?

B: Yes, how can I help?

A: Does this price include breakfast?

B: Yes, it does. The price includes breakfast.

—

A: If you want to check in now, you have to pay 40 dollars. And when you check out, you can pay the rest.

B: Why do I have to pay 40 dollars? What is that/the 40 dollars for?

A: It is a key deposit. When you check out, you will get the money back.

식당

A: 지금 오늘 밤으로 테이블 예약하는 게 가능할 거 같아요?

B: 잠시만요. 확인해 볼게요.

A: 몇 명이신가요? (=몇 명을 위해서요?)

B: 두 명이요.

A: 유감이지만, 우린 예약이 꽉 찼네요.

A: 저 뭔가 물어봐도 되나요?

B: 네. 어떻게 도와드릴 수 있을까요?

A: 이 가격이 아침식사를 포함하나요?

B: 네, 그래요. 그 가격은 아침식사를 포함합니다.

—

A: 지금 체크인 하시려면(=하고 싶으면), 40불 내셔야 돼요. 그리고 체크아웃 할 때, 나머지[the rest] 내시면 돼요.

B: 왜 40불을 내야 하죠? 그 40불은 뭘 위한 거죠?

A: 키 보증금[a key deposit] 이에요. 체크아웃 하실 때, 그 돈 돌려 받을 거예요.

Unit

6

형용사나 명사로 지난 상황을 말하고 싶을 때

형용사나 명사를 사용해 지난 상황을 말하고 싶을 때

be 동사 과거형 & when

동사가 아닌 형용사나 명사를 사용해서 지난 상황을 표현할 땐, am, is, are의
과거 형태인 was, were를 사용해요.

Positive (긍정)	Negative (부정)	Question (의문)
I He She It { was	I He She It { wasn't	Was { I? he? she? it?
You We They { were	You We They { weren't	Were { you? we? they?

<주의할 점>

-Be동사 현재형과 마찬가지로 be 동사는 '동사'이므로 다른 일반 동사와 한꺼번에 나열해서
사용하지 않아요!

예: I was go (x)

-주인공(주어)이 뚜렷하게 보이지 않고 애매할 때 = it

'비쌌어, 괜찮았어, 멀었어' 등의 경우 '그것'(우리가 지금 이야기하고 있는 그것)이 그렇다는 의미
이므로 매직워드인 it을 사용하면 됩니다.

이렇게 만듭니다!

형용사나, 명사를 be동사 뒤에 넣어 주기만 하면 돼요!

Positive (긍정)	Negative (부정)	Question (의문)
피곤했어. I was tired.	피곤하지 않았어. I wasn't tired.	피곤했니? Were you tired?

<심화 표현>

When을 과거를 표현하는 문장에서 사용하면, 한 시점에 일어난 두 가지 일을 표현할 수 있어서 활용도가 매우 높아요!

내가 어렸을 때,	When I was little,
내가 거기 있었을 때,	When I was there,
내가 전화했을 때,	When I called,
네가 왔을 때,	When you came,

예: 네가 왔을 때, 난 기분 좋았어.

When you came, I was happy.

긍정문 I was

☞ 오른쪽 힌트를 이용해서, 직접 문장을 만들어보세요!

훈련용 MP3

정답확인 : P 271

01	하루종일 집에 있었어. 🔊	
02	누워 있었어. 🔊	누워 있는 in bed
03	어젯밤에 너무 피곤했어. 🔊	너무 피곤한 exhausted
04	너무 배고팠어. 🔊	너무 배고픈 starving
05	작년 이맘때 난 홍콩에 있었어. 너무 좋았어. 🔊	작년 이맘때 this time last year
06	미안, 내가 일하느라 바빴어. 🔊	~하느라 바쁜 busy -ing
07	미안, 내가 바빴어 (서둘러야 했어). 🔊	바쁜 in a hurry
08	통화 중이었어요. 🔊	통화 중인 on the phone
09	회사 가는 길이었어. 🔊	가는 길 on the way (to)
10	며칠 전에 아팠어. 🔊	며칠 전 a few days ago/the other day

긍정문 I was

☞ 오른쪽 힌트를 이용해서, 직접 문장을 만들어보세요!

11	나도 어제 거기 있었는데. 🔊	
12	그 애 때문에 난 좀 짜증났었어. 🔊	짜증나는 annoyed, 그 애 때문에 because of him/her
13	그 애 혼자 있었어. 🔊	
14	걔네가 늦어서, 나 화났었어. 🔊	
15	난 너무 졸렸어. 그래서 잠들었어. 🔊	졸린 sleepy, 잠들다 fall asleep, fall-fell-fallen
16	나 너무 신났었어. 🔊	신나는, 기대되는 excited
17	너 운이 좋았어. 🔊	
18	난 네 편이었어. 난 항상 네 편이지. 🔊	너의 편 on your side
19	나 엄청 놀랐어. 🔊	놀란 surprised
20	그 애 엄청 떨었어. 🔊	떨리는,긴장되는 nervous

긍정문 It was

☞ 오른쪽 힌트를 이용해서, 직접 문장을 만들어보세요!

21	비쌌어. 🔊	
22	엄청 쉬웠어. 🔊	
23	똑같았어. 🔊	
24	이상했어. 🔊	
25	재미없었어. 🔊	재미없는 boring
26	젖어 있었어. 🔊	젖은 wet
27	미끄러웠어. 🔊	미끄러운 slippery
28	너무 멀었어. 🔊	
29	맛있었어요. 🔊	
30	그거 5분 전에 여기 있었는데. 이상하네. 🔊	

31	배가 안 고팠어. 그래서 별로 **안 먹었어.** 🔊	별로 much
32	**난 그 애랑 가깝지 않았어.** 🔊	가까운 close (to)
33	불행히도, 그 앤 운이 좋지 않았어. 🔊	불행히도 Unfortunately,
34	**나 짜증나지 않았었어.** 🔊	짜증나는 annoyed
35	난 아무것도 걱정하지 않았어. 🔊	
36	난 아무것도 무섭지 않았었어. 🔊	
37	나 답답하지 않았어. 🔊	답답한 frustrated
38	**기분 안 좋았어.** 🔊	기분 좋은 happy
39	난 만족하지 않았었어. 🔊	만족하는 satisfied
40	**슬프지 않았어. 난 괜찮았어.** 🔊	

부정문 It wasn't

☞ 오른쪽 힌트를 이용해서, 직접 문장을 만들어보세요!

41	그거 별로였어. (=안 좋았어.) 🔊	
42	편하지 않았어. 🔊	
43	어렵지 않았어. 하지만, 쉽지도 않았어. 🔊	도 either (부정문의 too)
44	어제 날씨 안 좋았어. 🔊	날씨 the weather
45	심각하지 않았어. 🔊	
46	힘들지 않았어요. 🔊	
47	그거 거기에 없었어. 🔊	
48	내 취향이 아니었어. 🔊	내 취향 my style/my cup of tea
49	너의 잘못이 아니었어. 🔊	잘못 fault
50	좋은 경험이 아니었어. 그게 다야. 🔊	경험 experience

의문문 Were you?

☞ 오른쪽 힌트를 이용해서, 직접 문장을 만들어보세요!

51	너 왜 늦었었어? 🔊	
52	어제 왜 화났었어? 🔊	
53	너 어디 있었어? 나 너 못 봤어. 🔊	
54	바빴니? 🔊	
55	넌 몇 살이었니? 🔊	
56	그게 좋은 선택이었어? 🔊	좋은 선택 a good choice
57	오해였어? 🔊	오해 a misunderstanding
58	사람 많았니? (복잡했니/붐볐니?) 🔊	사람 많은, 복잡한 crowded
59	그게 너의 결정이었어? 🔊	결정 decision
60	그게 너의 의도였니? 네 의도가 뭐였어? 🔊	의도 intention

의문문 Was it?

☞ 오른쪽 힌트를 이용해서, 직접 문장을 만들어보세요!

61	영화 어땠어? 좋았어? 🔊	
62	날씨 어땠어? 날씨 좋았어? 🔊	
63	너 자켓 너무 좋다! 비쌌니? 🔊	너무 좋다! I like
64	이거 얼마였어? 🔊	
65	오늘 하루 어땠어? 좋은 하루였니? 🔊	오늘 하루 your day
66	주말 어땠어? 🔊	주말 your weekend
67	멀었니? 얼마나 오래 걸렸어? 🔊	
68	너 생일이 언제였어? 🔊	
69	괜찮았니? 🔊	
70	재미있었어? 🔊	

When I was, I was

☞ 오른쪽 힌트를 이용해서, 직접 문장을 만들어보세요!

71	내가 어렸을 때, 난 수줍음을 많이 탔어. 🔊	어린 a child/a kid/little/a student, 수줍어하는 shy
72	내가 거기 있었을 때, 너도 거기 있었잖아. 🔊	
73	너가 아팠을 때, 네 걱정했어. 🔊	
74	내가 20살 때, 나 대담했어. 🔊	대담한, 용감한 bold
75	우리가 학생인 시절에, 우린 참 순진했지. 🔊	순진한 naive
76	내 동생이 10살 때, 엄청 귀여웠어. 🔊	
77	그 애가 어렸을 땐, 이기적이었어. 🔊	이기적인 selfish
78	내가 고등학생 때, 그게 유명했었어. 🔊	
79	우리가 아기 땐, 우린 항상 행복했었지. 🔊	
80	우리가 거기 있었을 때, 모두 (거기) 있었어. 🔊	

When I 과거, I was

☞ 오른쪽 힌트를 이용해서, 직접 문장을 만들어보세요!

81	내가 너한테 전화 했을 때, 너 바빴잖아.	
82	너가 왔을 때, 난 널 봐서 기뻤어.	오다 come-came-come
83	너가 그 애한테 말했을 때, 그 애 혼자였어?	말하다 tell-told-told
84	내가 그 애한테 물어봤을 때, 그 애 친절했어.	
85	내가 그 말 들었을 때, 나 충격 받았었어.	듣다 hear-heard-heard, 충격 받은 shocked
86	우리가 이거 찾았을 때, 우린 안도했었어.	찾다 find-found-found, 안도하는,다행인 relieved
87	내가 이겼을 때, 너무 행복했어.	이기다 win-won-won
88	너가 그거 잃어버렸을 때, 너 우울했었잖아.	잃어버리다 lose-lost-lost, 우울한 blue
89	너가 날 무시했을 때, 화났었어.	
90	너가 나한테 이거 줬을 때, 놀랐었어.	주다 give-gave-given

When I 과거, I was

☞ 오른쪽 힌트를 이용해서, 직접 문장을 만들어보세요!

91	나 어렸을 때, 개를 무서워했었어. 🔊	무서워하는 scared of/ afraid of
92	나 거기 갔을 때, 그게 처음이었어. 🔊	처음 my first time
93	나 집에 왔을 때, 너무 피곤했어. 🔊	오다 come-came-come
94	내가 그게 기억났을 때는, 너무 늦었었어. 🔊	
95	내가 전화했을 때, 너 (거기에) 없더라. 어디 있었어? 🔊	
96	우리가 도착했을 때, 아무도 (거기에) 없더라. 🔊	
97	그 애가 왔을 때, 난 밖에 있었어. 🔊	밖에 out
98	내가 이거 샀을 땐, 80불이었는데. 🔊	사다 buy-bought-bought
99	너가 그 애 봤을 때, 그 앤 어땠어? 🔊	보다 see-saw-seen
100	그런 일이 생겼을 때, 난 정말 놀랐었어. 🔊	정말 놀란 shocked

Positive (긍정)		Negative (부정)		Question (의문)	
I am -ing	해, 하고있어 (지금)	I'm not -ing	안 해, 안 하고있어	Are you -ing?	해? (지금) 하고 있어?
I 동사	해 (원래)	I don't	안 해	Do you?	해? (원래)
I will	할 걸, 할 거야 (예측)	I won't	안 할 걸, 안 할 거야	Will you?	할까? 할꺼야? (예측)
I think I'll	할 것 같아	I don't think I'll	안 할 것 같아	Do you think you'll	할 것 같아?
I may I might	할지도 몰라, 할 수도 있어	I may not I might not	안 할지도 몰라, 안 할 수도 있어	May I?	해도 돼요? (허락)
I 과거	했어, 했었어	I didn't	안 했어	Did you?	했어?

01	나 지금 뭔가 만들어야 돼서. 지금은 시간이 없어.	17	난 아무것도 안 만들거야. 난 모든 걸 주문할거야.
02	난 그 앨 위해 뭔가 만들고 싶어.	18	나 아무 것도 만들고 있지 않아. 난 벌써 다 끝났어.
03	생일 카드를 만들거야.	19	나 이거 안 만들었어. 샀어.
04	만드는 거 쉬워.	20	난 그거 못 만들어. 난 그거 잘 못 해. [잘하는 good at]
05	나 그거 만들 수 있어. 쉬워.	21	그거 이렇게 만들어줄래요? [이렇게 like this]
06	아무거나 만들어도 돼.	22	이거 왜 만들어야 돼요?
07	이번엔 작은 걸 만드는 게 좋겠어. [작은 거 a small one]	23	너가 이거 만들었을 때, 쉬웠어?
08	이거 다하고, 내가 그거 만들게.	24	이거 어떻게 만들어요?
09	지금 뭔가 만들고 있어서.	25	이거 어떻게 만들었어요?
10	나 그거 잘 만들어. 난 뭔가 만드는 거 잘해. [잘하는 good at]	26	이거 어디서 만들 수 있어요?
11	올해는 생일 케익을 내가 만들지도 몰라. 케익 만드는 법 배우고 있어. [~하는 법 how to]	27	뭐 만들거야? 우리 같이 해도 돼?
12	우리 이거 같이 만들지 뭐.	28	뭐 만들래?
13	나 이거 널 위해 만들었어. 맘에 들어? (=너 이거 좋아?)	29	우리 이거 같이 만들까?
14	우리 올해는 아무것도 안 만들지도 몰라.	30	우리가 뭘 만드는 게 좋을까?
15	만드는 거 어렵지 않아. 아무나 할 수 있어. [아무나 anyone]	31	뭐 만들고 있어?
16	난 그거 만들고 싶지 않아. 그냥 살래.	32	이거 너가 만들었어?

정답확인 : P 274

A: Hello. /Hi. I can't unlock the door. Can you help me?

B: Yes, I can help you with that. Can I (have a) look at your key? / Can I see your key?

A: Yes, this is my key. It is not working. / It doesn't work.

B: You are right. It isn't working. / It doesn't work. I will use mine. It is open.

A: Thank you for helping me. What should I do with this key?

B: When you go downstairs, I think you should give it to the front desk. When you tell them, they will give you a new key.

—

A: Hi. / Hello. My room key isn't working. / My room key doesn't work.

B: I am sorry (to hear that/ about that). Can you give me the key?

A: Here you are. / Here it is.

B: I will give you another key/ a new key.

A: Hello. / Hi. The AC/the air conditioning isn't working. / The AC doesn't work. It is too hot in the room.

B: I am so sorry. I will fix it right away.

A: Do you have other rooms? Can I have another room?

B: Ok. I will change the room for you.

Your new room number is 408, and this is the key. I am sorry for the inconvenience.

A: That's ok. Thank you for giving me a/the new room.

B: Thank you for understanding.

—

A: The shower isn't working. / The shower doesn't work. What should I do? / What do I do? / What shall I do?

B: I will send someone up right away.

A: I am sorry. The shower is working now. I didn't know how to use it. I turned this and it worked.

A: 안녕하세요. 문을 못 열겠어요. [열다(잠금을) unlock] 도와주실
래요?

B: 네, 제가 그거 도와드릴게요. 제가 당신의 키를 봐도 될까
요?

A: 네, 이게 제 키예요. 이거 안 돼요.

B: 당신 말이 맞네요. 이거 안 되네요. 제 것을 사용해 볼게요.
열렸네요.

A: 절 도와줘서 고마워요. [Thank you for-ing] 이 키로는 제가 뭘
하는게 좋을까요? [-로, -를 가지고 with]

B: 아래층에 내려가면, 프론트데스크에 주는 게 좋을 것 같아
요. 그들에게 말하면, 새 키를 줄거예요.

—

A: 안녕하세요. 제 방키가 안 돼요.

B: 죄송해요. 그 키 제게 주실래요?

A: 여기요.

B: 다른 키 드릴게요.

A: 안녕하세요. 에어컨이 안 돼요. 방안이 너무 더워요.

B: 죄송해요, 당장[right away] 시정할게요.

A: 다른 방 있어요? 다른 방으로 주세요.

B: 알겠어요. 당신을 위해서 방을 바꾸어 줄게요. 당신의 새로운 방번호는 408이고요, 이게 그 키에요. 불편하게 해드려 죄송합니다. [불편하게 해드려 the inconvenience]

A: 괜찮아요. 새로운 방 주셔서 감사해요.

B: 이해해주셔서 감사합니다.

—

A: 물이 안 나와요(=샤워가 안 돼요). 어떻하죠? (=전 뭘하죠?)

B: 당장 누군가를 위로 보낼게요.

A: 죄송해요. 샤워 되네요. 어떻게 사용하는 건지 몰랐어요. 이거 돌리니까, 됐어요.

A: I left my key in the/my room. What should I do?

B: Ok. I will open it for you. No problem.

—

A: I made a reservation online, but I forgot to bring my ticket.

B: That's ok. You don't have to have the ticket. Do you have reservation details on your phone?

A: Yes, I do. / Yes, I have them.

—

A: I lost my key. I can't find it.

B: I will open/unlock the door for you (for) now. If you can't find it in the room, (can you) let me know.

A: I paid a key deposit. What happens to the deposit?

B: If you lose the key, you will lose the deposit.

A: My/The wifi password isn't working. / The wifi password doesn't work. It is weird. It worked yesterday.

B: We change our/the password every day/ each day. This is today's password.

—

A: I gave you 20 dollars. And it is 15 dollars. But you only gave me 2 dollars.

A: You gave me the wrong amount.

A: The/My room is too small. Can I upgrade to a bigger room?

A: 제가 키를 방에 두고 왔어요. 어떻게하죠? (=뭘 하는게 좋을까요?)

B: 알겠어요. 제가 열어줄게요. 문제없어요.

—

A: 인터넷으로 예약을 했는데요, 제 티켓을 가져오는 것을 깜빡했어요.

B: 괜찮아요. 티켓 가지고 있지 않아도 돼요. 예약 정보[reservation details]가 휴대폰에 있나요?

A: 네, 있어요.

—

A: 저 키를 잃어버렸어요. 못 찾겠어요.

B: 지금은 제가 문을 열어 드릴게요. 방안에서 못 찾으면, 알려주세요.

A: 저 키 보증금을 냈는데요. 보증금은 어떻게 되는거죠? [어떻게 되는거죠? What happens to?]

B: 키를 잃어버리면, 보증금을 잃을 거예요.

A: 와이파이 비밀번호가 안 돼요 이상해요 어제는 됐는데요

B: 저희 매일 비밀번호를 바꾸어서요. 이게 오늘의 비번이에요.

—

A: 제가 20불 드렸어요. 이게 15불이고요. 근데 제게 2불만 주셨네요.

A: 제게 잘못 된 금액을 주셨어요.

A: 방이 너무 작아요. 더 큰 방으로 업그레이드 할 수 있을까요?

Unit

7

'그때' 하고 있던 걸 말하고 싶을 때

was, were + –ing '~하고 있었어'

지나간 어떤 시점에 하고 있었던 일에 대해 말하고 싶을 때 was, were -ing를 사용해요. 보통 ing가 들어가는 과거형의 문장은, 단순히 지난 과거를 얘기하는 것이 아니라, 그 특정 시점의 상황을 그림처럼 묘사하거나, 그때 하고 있던 행위 자체를 묘사하는 것에 초점이 맞추어져 있어요.

Positive (긍정)	Negative (부정)	Question (의문)
I He She It } was -ing	I He She It } wasn't -ing	Was { I he she it } -ing?
You We They } were -ing	You We They } weren't -ing	Were { you we they } -ing?
~하고 있었어 (그때)	~ 안 하고 있었어	~하고 있었어?

기초영어 1000문장 말하기 연습 2

이렇게 만듭니다!

Was, were를 사용하고, 동사 원형 뒤에 -ing를 넣습니다!

Positive (긍정)	Negative (부정)	Question (의문)
나 뭔가 하고 있었어. I was doing something.	나 아무것도 안 하고 있었어. I wasn't doing anything.	너 뭐 하고 있었어? What were you doing?
너가 전화했을 때, 운전하고 있었어. When you called, I was driving.	너가 전화했을 때, 나 운전하고 있던 거 아니었어. When you called, I wasn't driving.	내가 전화했을 때, 운전하고 있었어? When I called, were you driving?

\<함께 쓰는 단어\>

시간을 나타내는 표현: when, while, then

정답확인 : P 274

01	나 네 생각하고 있었어.	
02	미안, 나 다른 생각하고 있었어.	(뭔가) 다른 거 something else
03	나 막 나가려던 중이었어.	막 just
04	집에 가고 있었어.	
05	뭔가 하고 있었어.	
06	책 읽고 있었어.	
07	나 너 기다리고 있었어.	
08	고마워. 나 이거 찾고 있었는데. 어디서 찾았니?	찾다, 찾아보다 look for, 찾다 find
09	나 운동하고 있었어.	
10	나 너한테 문자하고 있었는데.	

긍정문 was/were -ing

☞ 오른쪽 힌트를 이용해서, 직접 문장을 만들어보세요!

11	우리 자고 있었어.	
12	그때 나 운전 중이었어.	
13	나 이거 쓰고 있었는데.	
14	요리 하고 있었어. 저녁 먹고 가.	저녁 먹고 가. Stay for dinner.
15	우리 방금 네 얘기 하고 있었는데.	
16	모두 널 응원하고 있었어.	응원하다 root for
17	모두 열심히 일하고 있었어.	
18	누군가 코골고 있었어. 너무 웃겼어.	코골다 snore
19	셀카 찍고 있었어.	
20	너 뭔가 보고 있었잖아. 뭐였어?	

긍정문 was/were -ing
☞ 오른쪽 힌트를 이용해서, 직접 문장을 만들어보세요!

21	내가 도착했을 때, Tim이 기다리고 있었어.	
22	너가 왔을 때, 난 TV 보고 있었어.	
23	그 애가 들어왔을 때, 우리는 그 애 얘기 하고 있었어.	
24	너가 벨 눌렀을 때, 샤워하는 중이었어.	벨 누르다 ring the (door)bell, ring-rang-rang
25	내가 그 애 봤을 때, 그 애 일하고 있었어. 바쁘던데.	
26	네가 전화했을 때, 나 네 생각하고 있었어.	
27	내가 널 기다리고 있을 때, 나 Jim 봤어.	
28	나 요리 하다가 (그때), 손을 베었어.	하다가 (그때) when/while
29	나 설거지하다가, 잔을 깼어.	설거지하다 wash the dishes
30	나 운동하다가, 다쳤어.	다치다 hurt oneself

31	비가 억수같이 쏟아지고 있었지. 🔊	비가 억수같이 쏟아지다, 엄청 내리다 rain cats and dogs
32	눈이 내리고 있었어. 모든 게 하얀색이었어. 너무 아름다웠어. 🔊	
33	그 애는 정말 예쁜 드레스를 입고 있었어. 멋져 보였어. 🔊	보이다 look, 멋진 hot/gorgeous
34	그는 검정 자켓을 입고 있었어. 🔊	
35	모두가 그냥 거기 서서, 아무 것도 안 하고 있었어. 🔊	서있다 stand
36	아무도 그걸 쓰고 있지 않아서, 내가 썼어. 🔊	
37	아무도 여기에 앉아 있지 않아서, 내가 가져왔어. 🔊	가져오다 bring-brought-brought
38	아무도 그걸 하고 있지 않아서, 내가 했어. 🔊	
39	아무도 그걸 보고 있지 않아서, 내가 껐어. 🔊	
40	아무도 이야기하고 있지 않아서, 엄청 조용했어. 🔊	

부정문 I wasn't -ing

☞ 오른쪽 힌트를 이용해서, 직접 문장을 만들어보세요!

41	괜찮아. 나 안 자고 있었어. 🔊	
42	아무것도 안 하고 있었어. 🔊	
43	아무데도 가고 있지 않았어. 🔊	
44	아무것도 생각 하고 있지 않았어. 🔊	
45	나 우는 거 아니었어. 🔊	
46	저 운전을 빨리 하고 있지 않았어요. 50으로 가고 있었는데. 🔊	운전 빨리 하다 speed
47	미안, 듣고 있지 않았어. 뭐라고 했니? 🔊	
48	미안, 난 그거 보고 있지 않았어. 🔊	
49	나 이거 쓰고 있지 않았어. 이거 가져가도 돼. 🔊	
50	우리 네 얘기 하고 있던 거 아니야. 🔊	

부정문 I wasn't -ing

☞ 오른쪽 힌트를 이용해서, 직접 문장을 만들어보세요!

51	너가 전화했을 때, 난 아무것도 안 하고 있었어.	
52	너 왔을 때, 나 일 안 하고 있었어.	
53	내가 아까 너 봤을 때, 나 가게에 가던 거 아니었어.	아까 earlier
54	잘 듣고 있지 않았어.	잘 듣다, 주의를 기울이다 pay attention (to)
55	알고보니, 내가 제대로 하고 있지 않았더라고.	알고보니 Turns out, 제대로 properly
56	나 아무 말도 안 하고 있었어.	
57	나 기분이 안 좋았어.	기분이 좋다 feel good
58	나 몸이 안 좋았어.	몸/컨디션이 좋다 feel well
59	그 애는 사실을 말하고 있지 않았어.	사실을 말하다 tell the truth
60	나 꾀병부리는 거 아니었어. 정말 아팠다고.	꾀병부리다, 가짜로 하다 fake

의문문 Were you -ing?

☞ 오른쪽 힌트를 이용해서, 직접 문장을 만들어보세요!

61	이거 쓰고 있었니?	
62	이거 듣고 있던거니?	
63	자고 있었니? 내가 널 **깨웠니?**	깨우다 wake-up
64	이거 보는 중이었니? (TV)	
65	일하고 있었어?	
66	누군가 기다리고 있었니?	
67	나 기다리고 있던 거니? 오래 **기다렸어?**	
68	뭔가 찾고 있었어? 그거 찾았어?	
69	뭐 찾고 있었어? 너가 말해주면, 내가 도와줄게.	
70	집에 가는 중이었니?	

71	어디 가던 길이었어?	
72	뭐하고 있었어?	
73	뭔가 하던 중이었니? 얘기할 시간 있어?	
74	내 얘기 하고 있었어?	
75	무슨 얘기 하고 있었어?	
76	운전 빨리 하고 있었니?	
77	얼마나 빨리 가고 있었니?	얼마나 빨리 how fast
78	무슨 생각을 하고 있던거야?	
79	왜 뛰고 있었어?	run-running
80	뭔가 요리하고 있었니?	

의문문 Were you-ing?

☞ 오른쪽 힌트를 이용해서, 직접 문장을 만들어보세요!

81	넌 거기서 뭐하고 있었어?	
82	그 앤 뭐하고 있었어?	
83	내가 무슨 말 하고 있었지?	
84	내가 뭐 하고 있었지?	
85	내가 뭘 찾고 있었더라?	
86	넌 어디 앉아 있었어?	
87	뭘 하려고 하던 거였어?	하려고 하다 try to
88	뭘 말하려던 거였어?	
89	너 누구랑 얘기하고 있었어?	
90	공부하고 있었어?	

의문문 Were you-ing?

☞ 오른쪽 힌트를 이용해서, 직접 문장을 만들어보세요!

91	내가 전화했을 때, 넌 뭐하고 있었어?	
92	너가 그 남자 봤을 때, 그 앤 뭐하고 있었어?	
93	너가 거기 갔을 때, 그 애가 기다리고 있었어?	
94	노래하고 있었니?	
95	뭐 연습하고 있었어?	
96	기분은 어땠어?	
97	너희 왜 싸우고 있었어?	싸우다 fight/argue
98	넌 왜 그 앨 피하고 있었어?	
99	뭘 숨기고 있었어?	숨기다 hide
100	왜 속삭이고 있었어?	속삭이다 whisper

Positive (긍정)		Negative (부정)		Question (의문)	
I am -ing	해, 하고있어 (지금)	I'm not -ing	안 해, 안하고있어	Are you -ing?	해? (지금) 하고 있어?
I 동사	해 (원래)	I don't	안 해	Do you?	해? (원래)
I will	할 걸, 할 거야 (예측)	I won't	안 할 걸, 안 할 거야	Will you?	할까? 할꺼야? (예측)
I think I'll	할 것 같아	I don't think I'll	안 할 것 같아	Do you think you'll	할 것 같아?
I may I might	할지도 몰라, 할 수도 있어	I may not I might not	안할지도 몰라, 안할 수도 있어	May I?	해도 돼요? (허락)
I 과거	했어, 했었어	I didn't	안 했어	Did you?	했어?
I was -ing	하고 있었어 (그때)	I wasn't -ing	안 하고 있었어	Were you -ing?	하고 있었어? (그때)

01	내가 운전할래.	17	너 이렇게 운전하면 안 돼.
02	내가 운전할 게.	18	우리 거기 차로 안 갈거야. 우리 기차타고 갈거야.
03	너가 원하면, 내가 운전할 수 있어.	19	난 운전 안 해도 돼.
04	우리 거기 운전해서 가야 돼. 너무 멀어.	20	나 운전 못 하겠어.
05	우리 운전해서 내려가는 게 좋을 것 같아. [운전해서 내려가다 drive down]	21	우리 거기 차로 안 갈 것 같아. 버스타고 갈지도 몰라.
06	나 거기 차로 갈거야. (운전해서)	22	내가 운전 안 했어. 그 애가 했어.
07	너가 괜찮다면, 너가 운전해도 돼.	23	운전 빨리하고 있지 않았는데.
08	지금 운전 중이라서. 내가 도착하자마자, 전화할게.	24	그 애 운전 안 해. 운전 면허증 없어.
09	우리 거기 차로 갈지도 몰라. (운전해서)	25	너가 운전해줄래?
10	너가 전화했을 때, 운전하고 있었어.	26	내가 운전해도 돼?
11	그 애 운전 잘 해.	27	거기 차로 갈거야?
12	우리 거기 차로 가지 뭐.	28	여기 차로 왔어? 얼마나 오래 걸렸어?
13	우리는 차로 갈 것 같아.	29	내가 전화했을 때, 운전하고 있었어?
14	거기 차로 가는 게 더 나아.	30	지금 운전하고 있어?
15	우리 거기 차로 갔었어. 한 시간 걸렸어.	31	넌 운전해? 차 있어?
16	난 운전 안 할래. 너무 피곤해.	32	넌 차로 갈 것 같아? 난 걸어갈 것 같아.

정답확인 : P 277

A: I want to go to Union Square. How can I get/go there from here?

B: How are you going to go/get there? Are you going to drive there?

A: Yes, I am going to drive there. The GPS/the navigation system isn't working. Is it far from here?

B: It isn't far. Do you have a map in the car?

A: I have no idea. / I don't know.

B: I think you should look (for it). They usually put maps in the car.

A: Yes, I will (do that).

B: You drive straight 3 blocks. Then, (you) turn right. And (then) you will see the sign.

A: How long does it take to go/get there? Will it take long?

B: It usually takes 20 minutes to go/get there. It might/may take long/longer because of the traffic (jam) now.

A: Thank you so much.

B: It will be easy to find.

B: How was your day? Did you like Union Square?

A: It was a good day. I loved/liked Union Square.

B: Was it easy to find?

A: Yes, it was easy to find.

B: How long did it take to get/go there? Did it take long?

A: It took 20 minutes.

A: Union Square에 가고 싶은데요. 여기서 어떻게 거길 갈 수 있어요?

B: 어떻게 거기 갈건데요? 운전해서 갈거예요?

A: 네, 운전해서 갈거예요. GPS(혹은 네비게이션 시스템)가 안 되네요. 여기서 먼가요?

B: 멀진 않아요. 차에 지도 있어요?

A: 모르겠어요.

B: 찾아 보는 게 좋을 것 같아요. 그들이 보통 시티 지도를 차안에 넣어두거든요.

A: 네, 그럴게요.

B: 3블록을 직진 하고요. 그리고 우회전해요. 그리고 나서는 사인이 보일 거예요.

A: 거기 가는데 얼마나 오래 걸려요? 오래 걸릴까요?

B: 거기 가는데 보통 20분 걸려요. 지금은 차 막혀서[because of the traffic (jam)]오래 걸릴지도 몰라요.

A: 정말 감사해요.

B: 찾기 쉬울 거예요.

B: 오늘 하루 어땠어요? Union Square 좋았어요? (누구??-너!!)

A: 좋은 하루였어요. Union Square 좋았어요.

B: 찾기 쉬웠어요?

A: 네, 찾기 쉬웠어요.

B: 거기 가는데 얼마나 오래 걸렸어요? 오래 걸렸어?

A: 20분 걸렸어요.

거리관련

A: Can I have a ticket to Rabbit Island, please?

B: The ferry leaves in 10 minutes.

A: How long will it take to get/go there from here?

B: It will take 40 minutes.

A: What time do you think I/we will arrive/get there?

B: It is almost/nearly 3. If it leaves on time, you will get/arrive there at 3: 40.

A: What did you do today? Did you do something special?

B: I went to a café in Gwacheon. I had a birthday party there.

A: Is it far from here? How did you go/get there?

B: It is a bit far from here. I drove there. We left early, so it didn't take long. When we got/arrived there, it was 5.

A: Did you have a good day?

B: I had a great/lovely/wonderful day.

거리관련

A: Rabbit Island행 티켓 한 장 주세요.

B: 페리가 10분 있다 출발하네요.

A: 여기서 거기 가는데 얼마나 걸릴까요?

B: 40분 걸릴거예요.

A: 거기에 몇 시에 도착할 것 같아요?

B: 지금이 거의 3시네요. 만약 제 시간에 출발한다면, 3시 40분

에 도착할 것 같아요.

—

A: 오늘 뭐 했어? 특별한 것[something special] 했니?

B: 과천에 있는 카페에 갔었어. 생일파티 거기에서 했어.

A: 여기서 멀어? 어떻게 갔었어?

B: 여기서 조금 멀긴해. 운전해서 갔었어. 우리 일찍 출발해서,

오래 걸리지 않았어. 거기 도착했을 때, 5시더라.

A: 좋은 하루 보냈어?

B: 정말 좋은 하루 보냈어.

Unit

8

과거에서 지금까지 연결된 일이나
경험을 말하고 싶을 때

과거에서 지금까지 연결된 일이나
경험을 말하고 싶을 때

have p.p. '~했어, 해봤어'

과거의 뉘앙스를 가지고 있지만, 현재에 속하는 문장은 have p.p.를 사용해서 말해요. 지금까지 살아오면서의 경험이나, 과거의 어느 시점부터 지금까지 쭉 연결된 일을 표현할 수 있어요.

Positive (긍정)		Negative (부정)		Question (의문)	
I We You They	have p.p.	I We You They	haven't p.p.	Have	I we you they	p.p?
He She It	has p.p.	He She It	hasn't p.p.	Has	he she it	p.p?
① 해봤어 [경험] ② 했어 [쭉, 계속] (~한지 ~됐어)		① 안 해봤어 ② 안 했어 [쭉, 계속] (~ 안 한지 ~됐어)		① 해봤어? ② 했어? [쭉, 계속] (~한지 ~됐어?)	

이렇게 만듭니다!

규칙동사는 -ed, 불규칙 동사는 Unit 0 세 번째 칸에 해당하는 단어를 have와 함께 사용해요!

Positive (긍정)	Negative (부정)	Question (의문)
나 거기 가봤어. [경험] I have been there.	나 거기 안 가봤어. I haven't been there.	너 거기 가봤어? Have you been there?
나 여기서 일한 지 3년 됐어. [쭉, 계속] I have worked here for 3 years.	나 여기서 일한 지 오래 되지 않았어. I haven't worked here for a long time.	여기서 일한 지 얼마나 오래됐어? How long have you worked here?

\<함께 쓰는 단어\>

시간을 나타내는 표현: recently, yet, how long, so far, for, since, before

\<비교분석\>

"Gone vs Been"

Gone	Been
갔다!	갔다 왔다! (가봤다! 와봤다!)

\<심화표현\> Since

Since는 '~때부터'라는 표현으로, when처럼 과거를 나타내는 문장과 함께 사용해요. 그때부터 지금까지 쭉 연결되는 의미를 가지고 있어서, have p.p.와 너무 잘 어울려요!

내가 어렸을 때부터	since I was little,
네가 왔을 때부터	since you came,

예: 내가 어렸을 때부터 여기서 살았어. Since I was little, I have lived here.

정답확인 : P 278

01	나 이거 전에 해봤어.	do-did-done
02	나 그 애 만나 본 적 있어.	meet-met-met
03	나 그거 들어 봤어.	hear-heard-heard
04	나 저분 본 적 있는데. 어딘지는 기억이 안 나.	see-saw-seen, 어딘지 where
05	나 이거 전에 써 봤어.	
06	우리 이거 먹어 봤잖아. 기억나?	먹어보다 try
07	생각해 봤어. 그리고, 가기로 했어.	think-thought-thought
08	나 그 영화 3번 봤어.	
09	우리 전에 만나 본 적 있어요. 작년이었죠.	
10	나 그거 읽어 봤어. 좋은 책이야.	read-read[red]-read[red]

11	나 은행 갔다 왔어. 🔊	
12	**우리 거기 여러 번 가 봤어.** 🔊	
13	나 여기 전에 와 봤어. 🔊	
14	**나 화장실 다녀왔어.** 🔊	
15	우리 여기 전에 몇 번 와 봤어요. 🔊	
16	**나 제주도 세 번 가 봤어. 난 제주도 좋아해.** 🔊	
17	그 애 일본에 많이 가 봤어. 그의 가족이 거기 있어. 🔊	
18	**그 앤 많은 나라에 가 봤어. 그 앤 여행을 많이 해.** 🔊	
19	저 여기 두 번 와 봤어요. 🔊	
20	**나 중국에 한 번 가 봤어. 작년에 갔었어. 다시 가고 싶어.** 🔊	

21	나 여기서 산지 3년 됐어.	3년 for 3years
22	나 2017년 부터 여기서 일했어.	2017부터 since 2017
23	우리 서로 안지 오래됐어요. 우리 2002년에 처음 만났어.	서로 each other
24	나 그거 가진지 한 6개월 됐어.	have-had-had
25	나 그 차 몰은지 오래됐지. 이제 새 차를 원해!	drive-drove-driven
26	나 아침에 일어났을 때부터, 머리가 아팠어.	머리아프다 have a headache
27	내가 20살 때부터, 이 순간을 원해왔어.	
28	그 애 한국에 온지(있은지) 2년 됐어. 2년 전에 한국에 왔어.	
29	나 이거 늘 갖고 싶었어. 내가 30살 됐을 때부터.	(나이가) 되다 turn
30	항상 만나고 싶었어요. 얘기(=너에 대해) 많이 들었어요. 만나서 정말 반가워요.	

31	우리 사귄지 3년 됐어. 🔊	사귀는 together
32	나 요즘 바빴어. 🔊	요즘 recently
33	나 계속 너 걱정했어. 🔊	걱정하는 worried about
34	(그거) 지금까진 좋았어. 🔊	지금까지 so far
35	나 잘 지냈어. 넌? 🔊	잘 있는 well
36	요새 계속 춥네. 🔊	
37	그 애 선생인지 오래됐어. 🔊	
38	우린 어렸을 때부터, 제일 친한 친구였어. 🔊	
39	그 애 병원에 있은지 일주일째야. 내일 그 애 보러 갈거야. 🔊	
40	너 아침내내 삐져있네. 뭐가 문제야? 🔊	삐진, 투덜대는 grumpy

41	생각해 본 적이 없어요. 🔊	think-thought-thought
42	이거 안 해봤어요. 그래서 어떻게 쓰는 건지 몰라요.	어떻게 쓰는 건지, 방법 how to use
43	이거 아직 안 써 봤어. 🔊	
44	나 그 애 몇 번 본 적 있는데, 얘기는 안 해봤어. 🔊	see-saw-seen, speak-spoke-spoken
45	나 이거 할 시간이 없었어. 🔊	
46	나 그 영화 아직 안 봤어. 같이 볼까? 🔊	
47	그 애 아직 안 왔어. 🔊	
48	그거 아직 도착 안 했어요. 언제 보냈어요? 🔊	
49	너가 날 위해 그거 사준 후로는, 난 다른 건 안 썼어. 🔊	다른 것 anything else
50	그 일이 있은 후로는, 나 그 애 못 봤어. 🔊	

부정문 I haven't been (to)

☞ 오른쪽 힌트를 이용해서, 직접 문장을 만들어보세요!

51	거기 아직 안 가 봤어. 🔊	
52	나 전에 여기 안 와 봤어. 처음이야. 🔊	(내) 처음 my first time
53	우리 제주도 아직 안 가 봤어. 🔊	
54	유럽 안 가 봤어. 🔊	
55	나 아직 우체국 안 갔다왔어. 시간이 없었어. 🔊	
56	우리 거기 안 가 본지 오래됐다. 오늘 거기 갈래? 🔊	
57	날씨가 요즘 계속 안 좋았어. 🔊	
58	그때 이후론, 그거 같지 않아. 모든 게 다르게 느껴져. 🔊	
59	그거 그렇게 오래되진 않았어. 한 5분 됐어. 🔊	그렇게 오래 that long
60	넌 제 시간인 적이 없어. 항상 늦어. 이번엔 너의 핑계가 뭐야? 🔊	핑계 excuse

부정문 I haven't p.p.

☞ 오른쪽 힌트를 이용해서, 직접 문장을 만들어보세요!

61	우리 서로 안 본지 오래됐다. 정말 오래됐다. 🔊	
62	나 운동 안 한지 몇 달 됐어. 🔊	
63	나 골프 안 친지 1년 됐어. 🔊	
64	나 여기서 일한지 오래되지 않았어. 작년 12월에 시작했어. 🔊	
65	나 그거 안 한지 오래됐다. 🔊	
66	아침 이후로 아무것도 안 먹었어. 🔊	아침 이후로 since breakfast
67	여기 온지(있은지) 오래 안 됐어. 5분 전에 도착했어. 🔊	
68	나 그 애랑 연락 안 한지 몇 달 됐어. 🔊	연락하다 speak to
69	그(때) 이후론 (난) 아무 문제 없었어. 🔊	없다 = 가지고 있지 않다, 그 이후로 since then
70	그 애 아직 안 나갔어. 아직 (여기) 있어.	아직, 아직도, 여전히 still

의문문 Have you p.p.?

☞ 오른쪽 힌트를 이용해서, 직접 문장을 만들어보세요!

71	우리 전에 만난 적 있었나요? 낯익어 **보여요**.	낯익은 familiar
72	이 책 읽어 봤어?	
73	생각해봤니? 너의 결정이 뭐야?	결정 decision
74	이거 많이 해봤어? 너무 잘 한다!	
75	몇 번 해봤어?	몇번 how many times
76	차 키 찾는데. (그게) 어디 갔지? 봤어?	
77	이거 먹어 봤어? 정말 맛있어.	
78	이거 사용해 본 적 있어? 어떻게 쓰는지 알아?	
79	내가 너한테 몇 번을 말했어? 이거 아직 하면 안 돼. 때가 아니야.	때 the time
80	한국에 온지(있은지) 얼마나 됐어요? 한국말 잘 하시네요!	

81	어디 갔다왔어? 나 너 찾았잖아.(= 찾고 있었어)	
82	우체국에 갔다왔니?	
83	이 식당에 와 본 적 있니?	
84	호주 가 봤어?	
85	전에 여기 와 본적 있어요? 처음이에요?	
86	부산 가 봤어요?	
87	오랜만이야. 잘지냈어? 어떻게 지냈어?	
88	요즘 바빴니?	
89	아팠니? 아픈지 얼마나 오래됐어?	
90	오늘 하루 어땠어? (지금까지)	오늘 하루 your day

91	여기서 일한지 얼마나 오래됐어?	
	🔊	
92	거기서 산지 오래됐어?	
	🔊	
93	얼마나 오래됐니?	
	🔊	
94	여기 온지(있은지) 오래됐니? 언제 왔어?	
	🔊	
95	결혼한지 얼마나 오래됐어요?	결혼한 married
	🔊	
96	(이거) 이런지 얼마나 오래됐어요?	이런지 like this
	🔊	
97	너 그거 안지 얼마나 됐어?	
	🔊	
98	작가인지 얼마나 오래됐어요?	
	🔊	
99	너희 서로 안지 얼마나 됐어?	
	🔊	
100	그 애가 너의 절친인지 얼마나 오래됐어?	
	🔊	

Positive (긍정)		Negative (부정)		Question (의문)	
I am -ing	해, 하고있어 (지금)	I'm not -ing	안 해, 안하고있어	Are you -ing?	해? (지금) 하고 있어?
I 동사	해 (원래)	I don't	안 해	Do you?	해? (원래)
I will	할 걸, 할 거야 (예측)	I won't	안 할 걸, 안 할 거야	Will you?	할까? 할꺼야? (예측)
I think I'll	할 것 같아	I don't think I'll	안 할 것 같아	Do you think you'll	할 것 같아?
I may I might	할지도 몰라, 할 수도 있어	I may not I might not	안할지도 몰라, 안할 수도 있어	May I?	해도 돼요? (허락)
I 과거	했어, 했었어	I didn't	안 했어	Did you?	했어?
I was -ing	하고 있었어 (그때)	I wasn't -ing	안 하고 있었어	Were you -ing?	하고 있었어? (그때)
I have p.p.	① 해봤어 (경험) ②했어 (쭉, 지금까지)	I haven't p.p.	①안 해봤어 ②안 했어 (계속)	Have you p.p.?	①해봤어? ②했어? (계속)

01	안경 없이도 그거 읽을 수 있어.	23	난 책 안 읽어. 읽을 시간이 없어.
02	안경 없이 그거 읽고 싶어.	24	나 책 안 읽은지 오래됐어.
03	너 그거 읽어 봐야 돼. 좋은 책이야.	25	아무것도 읽고 있지 않았어.
04	이거 읽어 봐도 돼. 내 허락 필요없어. [내 허락 my permission]	26	나 네 일기 안 읽었어.
05	이번달엔 우리 이 책을 읽는 게 좋을 것 같아요.	27	나 이거 읽어봐도 돼?
06	내가 먼저 읽어 보고, 알려줄게.	28	이거 읽어줄래?
07	이 책 읽기 어려워.	29	이번달엔 어느 책 읽을까?
08	난 책 읽을 거야.	30	뭐 읽을래?
09	이 책 읽지 뭐.	31	넌 독서하니? 난 책 안 읽어.
10	나 지금 책 읽어.	32	우리 이거 읽어 보는 게 좋을까?
11	그 앤 (책) 많이 읽어. 책을 좋아해.	33	뭐 읽고 있어?
12	나 그거 저번달에 읽었어. 좋았어.	34	내가 왔을 때, 너 뭔가 읽고 있었잖아. 뭐 읽고 있었어?
13	나 그 책 읽어봤어. 괜찮았어.	35	뭔가 읽고 있니? 뭐 읽어?
14	너 왔을때, 난 이 책 읽고 있었어. 꽤 흥미 로워. [꽤 pretty/quite, 흥미로운 interesting]	36	이 책 읽어 봤어?
15	너 이거 읽으면 안 돼. 내 일기장이야.		
16	나 이거 못 읽겠어. 눈이 피곤해.		
17	나 아무것도 읽고 싶지 않아.		
18	너 이거 안 읽어도 돼. 내가 읽어줄게.		
19	그 애 책 안 읽을지도 몰라. 책 안 좋아해.		
20	아무것도 읽고 있지 않아.		
21	나 그거 아직 안 읽어 봤어.		
22	너 허락 없이는 안 읽을게.		

정답확인 : P 281

가격 관련

A: How much is it altogether?

B: It is 250 dollars altogether. How would you like to pay? / How do you want to pay?

A: I will pay cash. If I pay cash, can you give me a discount?

B: I am sorry. The items are all on sale. / All of the items are on sale. It isn't possible to give you a discount.

—

A: How much will the total be? Will it be expensive?

B: I don't think it will be expensive. Our price is the best. The total will be 320 dollars.

A: Do you take/accept credit cards?

B: Yes, we take visa and master cards.

—

A: I'd like to try this tour. How much does it cost to do this tour?

B: It costs 45 dollars. But, if you want to add/include other activities, it will cost more.

A: If I add/include this horse riding experience, how much will it cost?

B: The horse riding experience usually costs 25 dollars. If you want to add this to the tour, it will be cheaper. I will check the price. It will cost 65 dollars altogether.

A: 이거 다 해서 [altogether] 얼마예요?

B: 다 해서 250불이에요. 어떻게 지불하실래요?

A: 현금으로 낼게요. 현금내면, 할인해 줄 수 있나요?

B: 죄송해요. 이 아이템들이 모두 세일 품목(on sale)이라서요.
     할인 해드리는 게 가능하지 않아요.

—

A: 전부 다 [the total] 얼마일까요? 비쌀까요?

B: 비쌀 것 같지 않아요. 저희 가격이 최고예요. 전부다 320불일
     거예요.

A: 신용카드 받으세요?

B: 네, 저희 비자랑 마스터 카드 받아요.

—

A: 이 투어 해보고 싶은데요. 이 투어 하는데 얼마 드나요?

B: 45 불 들어요. 하지만, 다른 활동을 추가 하고[add/include] 싶
     으시면, 더 들거예요.

A: 제가 이 말타기(horse riding) 경험을 추가한다면, 얼마 들까요?

B: 말타기 경험은 원래 25불인데요. 만약 이걸 투어에 추가 하고 싶으면, 더 쌀거예요. [더 싼 cheaper] 가격 확인해 볼게요. 다 해 서 65불 들겠네요.

Dialogue Practice

A: My phone is not working. (My phone doesn't work.) Can you have/take a look (at it)?

B: Yes, I will take/have a look.

A: Will it be possible to fix?

B: Yes, it is possible to fix.

A: It is a bit urgent. I can't do anything without my phone. How long do you think it'll take?

B: I don't think it'll take very long. Our technician will be here soon.

A: How much will it cost to fix this? Do you think it'll cost a lot?

B: It depends. But, it doesn't look serious. I don't think it'll cost much.

A: Thank you. What do I do now?

B: Can you write your name and contact details/information here?

A: Yes, I will (do that).

B: Our technician is here. When it is ready, we will contact you.

A: Have you fixed your phone? / (Did you fix your phone?)

B: Yes, I have (fixed my phone). / Yes, I did. (I fixed it) It is working now.

A: How much did it cost to fix? Did it cost a lot?

B: It cost 30 dollars.

—

A: It looks new. Is it new?

B: Yes, it is a new one. / It is new.

A: How much was it?

B: I don't want to say. / I wouldn't like to say.

A: Why not? How much did you pay for it?

B: I paid 600 dollars (for it).

A: 제 전화가 안 돼요. 한 번 봐주실래요?

B: 네 봐드릴게요.

A: 제 전화가 안 돼요. 한 번 봐주실래요?

B: 네 봐드릴게요.

A: 고치는 게 가능할까요?

B: 네, 고치는 거 가능합니다.

A: 이게 좀 급한데요. 제 전화 없이는 아무것도 못 해요. 얼마나 오래 걸릴 것 같아요?

B: 별로 오래 안 걸릴 것 같아요. 저희 기술자[technician]가 금방 올거예요.

A: 이거 고치는데 얼마 들까요? 많이 들 것 같아요?

B: 상황에 따라 달라요. [It depends.] 하지만, 이건 심각하지 않은 걸로 보여요. 얼마(별로) 안 들 것 같아요.

A: 감사합니다. 이제 전 뭘 하죠?

B: 여기 카드에 이름하고 연락처[contact details/contact information] 적어주실래요?

A: 네, 그럴게요.

B: 기술자 분 왔네요. 다 되면, 연락드릴게요.

A: 너 폰 고쳤어?

B: 어 고쳤어. 이제 돼.

A: 고치는데 얼마 들었어? 많이 들었니?

B: 30불 들었어.

—

A: 이거 좋아 보이는데. 새 거니?

B: 어 새 거야.

A: 얼마였어?

B: 말하고 싶지 않아.

A: 왜? 얼마 주고 샀는데?

B: 600불 주고 샀어.

Unit

9

할 수 있었던 걸 말하고 싶을 때

could '~할 수 있었어'

Can의 과거 표현인 could는 무언가를 할 수 있었던 걸 말하고 싶을 때 사용해요. 특히, **부정문에서** couldn't는 무언가 할 수 없었던 것, 즉 '**~ 못 했어**'라는 표현에 사용되어 활용도가 매우 높아요.

하지만 의문문에서 could는 과거의 의미를 갖지 않고, can과 의미가 같아요!

Positive (긍정)	Negative (부정)	Question (의문)
I could	I couldn't	Could **you?**
		~해줄래요? [부탁]
~할 수 있었어	~ 못 했어, 할 수 없었어	Could **I?**
		~해도 돼요? [허락]

이렇게 만듭니다!

문장의 핵심단어인 '동사'를 넣습니다!

Positive (긍정)	Negative (부정)	Question (의문)
그거 쉽게 할 수 있었어. I could do it easily.	그거 못 했어. 미안. I couldn't do it. I'm sorry.	이거 해도 되나요? Could I do it?

"Can vs Could"

Can	Could
Can I? ~해도 돼요? 친근한 허락의 요청	Could I? ~해도 돼요? 약간 격식 있는 허락의 요청
Can you? ~해줄래요? 친근한 부탁	Could you? ~해줄래요? 약간 격식 있는 부탁

"Can vs Could vs May"

Can I?	~해도 돼요? [친근한 표현]
Could I?	~해도 돼요? [약간 격식 있는 표현]
May I?	~해도 돼요? [정중한 표현]

정답확인 : P 282

01	내가 어렸을 땐, 아주 빨리 잘 뛸 수 있었는데.	
02	피아노를 아주 잘 칠 수 있었지.	
03	내가 20대 땐, 나도 그거 할 수 있었어.	20대 in one's 20s
04	몇 년 전엔 술을 밤새도록 마실 수 있었어.	몇 년 전 a few years ago
05	나 타이핑 엄청 빨리 할 수 있었는데.	타이핑 하다 type
06	그 사건 전엔 그 애 수영을 정말 잘 할 수 있었어. 정말 활동적이었어.	그 사건 전 before the incident
07	그 사고 전엔 그는 테니스를 하루종일 칠 수 있었어.	사고 accident
08	우리가 학생일 땐, 우리 매일 어울릴 수 있었는데.	어울리다 hang out
09	아무도 그 앨 말릴 수 없었어. 고집이 셌어.	말리다 stop, 고집 센 stubborn
10	아무것도 내 마음을 바꿀 수 없었어.	

부정문 I couldn't

☞ 오른쪽 힌트를 이용해서, 직접 문장을 만들어보세요!

11	어제 아무것도 못 했어. 너무 피곤했거든.	
12	그 애는 못 왔어.	
13	미안, 내가 어제 못 왔어. 시간이 없었어.	
14	유감이지만, 다 못 했어요.	
15	아무한테도 말 못 했어.	
16	아무말도 못 했어.	
17	난 그거 못 믿겠더라고. (세상에, 황당했어)	
18	여기다가 아무것도 못 적었어요. 여기 뭘 써야 해요?	
19	어젯밤에 너무 피곤했어. 근데, 잠을 전혀 못 잤어.	전혀 at all
20	너무 피곤했어. 그래서, 오늘 아침에 일찍 못 일어났어.	

부정문 I couldn't

☞ 오른쪽 힌트를 이용해서, 직접 문장을 만들어보세요!

21	알람도 못 들었어. 🔊	~도, 조차도 even, 듣다 hear
22	나 어제 Jim 봤는데, 그 애한테 말 못 했어. 🔊	
23	네 전화번호를 찾을 수가 없었어. 그래서 전화 못 했어. 🔊	
24	숙제 못 했어. 시간이 없었어요. 🔊	
25	그 남자 말 너무 빨리해서, 못 알아들었어. 🔊	말 빨리하다 speak (so) fast, 알아듣다 understand
26	아무것도 못 먹었어. 아무것도 먹고 싶지 않았어. 🔊	
27	사진 못 찍었어. 🔊	
28	그땐 영어를 전혀 못 했어. 🔊	
29	아무것도 못 찾았어. 너무 답답했어. 🔊	답답한 frustrated
30	움직일 수가 없었어. 🔊	

31	미안해. 널 못 도와줘서. 🔊	
32	고를 수가 없었어. 난 다 좋았어. 🔊	
33	그거 못 샀어. 지갑을 집에 두고 갔었거든. 🔊	
34	난 그 애 못 알아봤어. 그 애 너무 달라 보였어. 🔊	알아보다 recognize
35	그거 못 썼어. 어떻게 쓰는 건지 몰라. 🔊	어떻게 쓰는 건지 how to use
36	아무것도 못 샀어. 뭘 살지 모르겠더라고. 🔊	뭘 살지 what to buy
37	결정 못 했어. 뭘 할지 모르겠어. 🔊	뭘 할지 what to do
38	어디로 갈지 결정 못 했어. 🔊	어디로 갈지 where to go
39	말 한마디 못 했어. 뭘 말할지 몰랐어. 🔊	말 한마디 a word, 뭘 말할지 what to say
40	가만히 있을 수가 없었어. 🔊	가만히 있다 stay still

부정문 I couldn't

☞ 오른쪽 힌트를 이용해서, 직접 문장을 만들어보세요!

41	그거 못 가져왔어요. 너무 무거웠어요. 🔊	
42	난 그를 이해 못 하겠더라고. 🔊	
43	울음을 멈출 수가 없었어. 🔊	멈추다 stop -ing
44	너무 웃겨서, 웃음을 멈출 수가 없었어. 🔊	웃다 laugh
45	너무 행복했어. 웃음을 멈출 수가 없었어. 🔊	웃다, 미소짓다 smile
46	우리 못 이겼어. 우리가 졌어. 🔊	지다 lose-lost-lost
47	잠을 잘 못 잤어. 너무 피곤하다.	
48	그 앨 용서할 수가 없었어. 🔊	
49	집중 못 했어. 너무 시끄러웠어. 🔊	
50	나 그 애 설득 못 했어. 어쩔 수 없지 뭐. 🔊	설득하다 persuade, 어쩔 수 없지 뭐. Never mind.

51	난 거짓말 못 하겠더라고. 🔊	
52	**알아내지 못 했어.** 🔊	알아내다 find out
53	아무것도 기억 안 나더라. (기억 못 했어) 🔊	
54	**이거 못 외웠어. 어려워!** 🔊	외우다 memorize
55	너무 화가났었어. 진정할 수가 없었어. 🔊	너무 화난 furious, 진정하다 calm down
56	**그걸 살 여유가 없었어.** 🔊	살/할 여유가 있다 afford
57	그거 해결하지 못 했어. 그냥 흘려 버릴거야. 🔊	흘려 버리다, 잊다, 내려 놓다 let-go
58	**(내 스스로) 즐기지 못 했어. 내 마음이 다른 데 있었어.** 🔊	다른 데 somewhere else /elsewhere
59	그땐 내 자신을 사랑할 수 없었어. 🔊	
60	**너한테 전화 못 했어. 미안해.** 🔊	

의문문 Could you?

☞ 오른쪽 힌트를 이용해서, 직접 문장을 만들어보세요!

61	이것 좀 해주실래요? 🔊	
62	부탁 좀 들어주실래요? 🔊	부탁 들어주다 do me a favor
63	저희한테 10분 있다가 다시 전화 해주실래요? 🔊	
64	더 일찍 와주실래요? 🔊	더 일찍 earlier
65	그거 다시 말해 주실래요? 🔊	다시 말하다 say-again/repeat
66	말 천천히 해주실래요? 🔊	말 천천히 하다 speak slowly
67	그거 가져와 주실래요? 🔊	
68	잠깐만 기다려주실래요? 🔊	
69	저한테 이메일 보내주실래요? 🔊	
70	결정하면, 저한테 알려주실래요? 🔊	

의문문 Could you?

☞ 오른쪽 힌트를 이용해서, 직접 문장을 만들어보세요!

71	저 기다려 주실래요?	
72	다른 것 좀 제게 보여주실래요?	다른 것 something else
73	조금만 옆으로 가주실래요?	옆으로 가다 move over
74	그걸 제게 설명해주실래요?	설명하다 explain -to
75	이거 어떻게 쓰는 건지 제게 보여주실래요?	어떻게 쓰는 건지 how to use
76	이거 어떻게 하는 건지 제게 가르쳐주실래요?	가르쳐주다 teach
77	이것 좀 도와주실래요?	~를 도와주다 help-with
78	다시 한 번 확인해주실래요?	다시 한 번 확인하다 double check
79	제 손을 잡아줄래요?	
80	제 전화 좀 건네줄래요?	건네주다 hand

의문문 Could I ?
☞ 오른쪽 힌트를 이용해서, 직접 문장을 만들어보세요!

81	저기 앉아도 되나요? 🔊	
82	저 지금 가도 될까요? 🔊	
83	제가 뭔가 물어봐도 되나요? 🔊	
84	개인적인 질문 해도 되나요? 🔊	
85	매니저랑 통화할 수 있나요? 🔊	
86	저 이거 가져가도 되나요? 🔊	
87	나중에 결정해도 되나요? 결정하자마자, 전화할게요.	
88	우리 다른 얘기해도 될까요? 🔊	다른 거 something else
89	우리 다음 주 중 만날 수 있을까요? 🔊	다음 주 중 sometime next week
90	우리 화제를 바꿔도 될까요? 그거에 대해 얘기하고 싶지 않아. 🔊	화제 바꾸다 change the subject

91	제가 오늘 저녁에 가지러 가도 되나요?	가지러 가다 pick-up
92	그거 내일 가져다 드려도 될까요?	가져다주다 drop-off
93	제가 시간을 가지고 생각해봐도 되나요? 시간이 더 필요해요.	
94	이번엔 제가 골라도 되나요? 이번엔 내가 고를래.	
95	제 폰이 죽었어요. (배터리 없음) 너의 폰 좀 사용해도 돼요?	죽은 dead
96	너희의 샘플들을 볼 수 있을까요?	
97	이 안이 조금 더워요. 이거 열어놔도 되나요?	열어놓다 leave-open
98	물 좀 주세요.	
99	앞접시 주세요.	앞접시 a plate/an extra plate
100	제가 오늘 할 일이 많아서요.(=할 걸 많이 가지고 있다) 다음번을 기약해도 될까요?	다음번을 기약하다 take a rain check

복습강의 MP3

Positive (긍정)		Negative (부정)		Question (의문)	
I am -ing	해, 하고있어 (지금)	I'm not -ing	안 해, 안하고있어	Are you -ing?	해? (지금) 하고 있어?
I 동사	해 (원래)	I don't	안 해	Do you?	해? (원래)
I will	할 걸, 할 거야 (예측)	I won't	안 할 걸, 안 할 거야	Will you?	할까? 할꺼야? (예측)
I think I'll	할 것 같아	I don't think I'll	안 할 것 같아	Do you think you'll	할 것 같아?
I may I might	할지도 몰라, 할 수도 있어	I may not I might not	안할지도 몰라, 안할수도 있어	May I?	해도 돼요? (허락)
I 과거	했어, 했었어	I didn't	안 했어	Did you?	했어?
I was -ing	하고 있었어 (그때)	I wasn't -ing	안 하고 있었어	Were you -ing?	하고 있었어? (그때)
I have p.p.	① 해봤어 (경험) ②했어 (쭉, 지금까지)	I haven't p.p.	①안 해봤어 ②안 했어 (계속)	Have you p.p.?	①해봤어? ②했어? (계속)
I could	할 수 있었어 (능력)	I couldn't	못 했어	Could you? Could I?	해줄래요? 해도 돼요?

01	난 그거 대신 이걸로 쓸래. [~대신 instead of]	23	난 그거 안 써. 난 내거 있어.
02	너 이걸로 써야 돼.	24	나 그거 쓰고 있지 않았어. 내거 쓰고 있었는데.
03	나 이걸로 쓰는 게 좋겠어.	25	나 그거 전혀 못 썼어. 쓸모없었어. [쓸모없는 useless]
04	이거로 쓰는 게 더 쉬워. [더 쉬운 easier]	26	이번엔 어느 걸로 쓸 것 같아?
05	이걸로 쓸게요.	27	우리 어느걸로 쓰는 게 좋을 것 같아?
06	너 내걸로 써도 돼요.	28	여기에 어느걸로 써야 돼요?
07	나 이거 쓸 수 있어. 이거 쓰는 법 (어떻게 쓰는지) 알아.	29	그거 말고(대신) 이걸로 써줄래요?
08	난 이걸로 쓸거야.	30	이거 쓰고 있었어요?
09	우리 이걸로 쓰지 뭐.	31	이거 전에 써봤어?
10	나 그거 써봤어. 사용하기 쉬워.	32	저 이거 써도 되나요?
11	저 그거 지금 쓰는 거예요.	33	이거 쓰고 있는 거예요? 아님 제가 가져가 도 되나요?
12	난 보통 이걸로 써.	34	어느 걸로 쓸거야?
13	나 그거 어젯밤에 썼어.	35	이거 얼마나 오래 썼어?
14	저 그거 쓰고 있었어요.	36	넌 어느 브랜드 써?
15	저 이거 쓴지 3년 됐어요.		
16	나 이거 못 쓰겠어. 이거 어떻게 쓰는 건 지 보여 줄래요?		
17	여기서 폰 쓰면 안 돼.		
18	나 지금 그거 안 써. 너가 써도 돼.		
19	그 애 이거 안 쓸지도 몰라. 새거 샀어.		
20	이거 사용 안 한지 오래됐어.		
21	이거 안 써봤어요. 사용하기 쉬운가요?		
22	나 그거 안 썼는데.		

정답확인 : P 284

일상

A: Long time no see. We haven't seen each other for a long time. How long has it been?

B: That's right. / You're right. It has been too long. We last saw each other a few years ago. How have you been?

A: I have been well/good. What/How about you? Have you been busy recently?

B: Same old, same old. I have been busy. I haven't had time to do anything recently.

A: I have a lot (of things) to tell you.

B: How is your boyfriend? Is he well?

A: He is well. We have already been together for 5 years.

B: Are you going to get married?

A: We (have) decided to get married next year.

B: Congratulations! I am so happy for you.

A: I want to hear about you now. / I'd like to hear about you now.

B: I have decided to travel more from this year. You have been to many countries. I haven't even been to Jeju island. I have been too busy. But I am going to make time now.

A: That's a great idea. I love travelling, too.

B: Have you been to Taiwan?

A: Yes, I have been to Taiwan. I went there a couple of years ago.

B: I might/may go there this summer. How was it?

A: It is a nice place. I had a great time there. I didn't want to come back.

B: How long did you stay (there)?

A: I stayed (there) for 4 days. I think you will like it there.

B: It was so good to see you. It is always good to talk to you.

A: It was good to see you, too. Keep in touch! / Stay in touch!

일상

A: 오랜만. 우리 서로 안 본지 너무 오래됐다. 얼마나 오래됐지?

B: 맞아. 너무 오래됐다. 우리 몇 년전에 마지막으로 봤었지. 어떻게 지냈어?

A: 난 잘 지냈어. 넌? 요즘 바빴니?

B: 늘 같지 뭐. [Same old, same old.] 바빴어. 요즘 아무것도 할 시간이 없어.

A: 너한테 할 말이 많아. (=할 말이 많이 있어)

B: 네 남자친구는 어때? 잘 지내?

A: 잘지내. 우리 벌써 사귄지 5년 됐어.

B: 결혼할거야?

A: 내년에 결혼하기로 했어.

B: 축하해. 너무 잘됐다. [I am so happy for you.]

A: 이제 너에 대해 듣고 싶어.

B: 난 올해부터는 여행을 더 하기로 했어. 넌 여러 나라 가봤잖아. 난 아직 제주도도 안 가봤어. 너무 바빴지. 하지만 이제 시간을 만들거야.

A: 좋은 생각이다. 나도 여행하는 거 좋아해. [like/love -ing]

B: 대만 가봤어?

A: 어, 나 대만 가봤어. 2년 전에 갔었어. [2년 전 a couple of years ago]

B: 이번 여름에 거기 갈지도 몰라. 어땠어?

A: 괜찮은 곳 이야. 거기서 좋은 시간 보냈어. 돌아오기 싫더 라고.

B: 얼마나 있었는데?

A: 4일 있었어. 너가 거기 좋아할 것 같아.

B: 오늘 봐서 너무 좋았어. 너랑 얘기하는 거 항상 좋아.

A: (나도) 널 봐서 너무 좋았어. 연락해. [Keep in touch!/Stay in touch!]

_____ 일상

A: Good morning. How was your weekend? Did you have a good weekend?

B: It was so good. I had a nice weekend.

A: What did you do?

B: I went to the East Sea to see a sunrise and eat some seafood.

A: How was the East Sea?

B: It was great. I saw a beautiful sunrise, and had raw fish.

A: I haven't been to the East Sea for a long time.

B: How was your weekend? Did you have a nice weekend?

A: It was a quiet weekend. I stayed at home, and slept nearly all day. It was relaxing.

B: What are you going to do this weekend? Do you have (any) plans?

A: I don't have (any) plans.

B: Shall we go to the movies? I want to see a movie.

A: Sounds good! I haven't been to the movies for a long time. It is going to be fun. / It will be fun.

일상

A: 좋은 아침! 주말 어땠어? 좋은 주말 보냈어?

B: 너무 좋았어. 정말 좋은 주말을 보냈어.

A: 뭐했어?

B: 나 동해에 일출도 보고, 해산물 먹으러 갔었어.

A: 동해 어땠어?

B: 아주 좋았어. 아름다운 일출도 보고, 회[raw fish] 먹었어.

A: 동해 안 가 본지 오래됐다.

B: 너의 주말은 어땠어? 좋은 주말 보냈어?

A: 조용한 주말이었어. 집에 있으면서, 거의 하루종일 잤어. 편했

어.[relaxing]

B: 이번 주말에 뭐 할거야? 약속(=계획) 있어?

A: 약속 (계획) 없어.

B: 영화보러 갈까? 영화 보고 싶어.

A: 좋아! [Sounds good!] 나 극장 안 가본지 오래 됐어. 재미있겠다.

Unit

10

상대의 입장에서 의견이나
조언을 말하고 싶을 때

상대의 입장에서 의견이나 조언을 말하고 싶을 때

would '(나라면) ~할 거야'

Will의 과거표현으로 많이 알고 있는 would는 '상상'을 표현하는 단어예요. 따라서 상대의 입장에서 내 의견을 전달하거나, 내 입장에서 상대의 조언을 구할 때 유용하게 쓰입니다.

'만약' 그렇다면, '만약' 나였다면 처럼, would는 진실이나 팩트를 말할 때 쓰는 단어가 아니기 때문에, 구별을 위해 **과거형으로** 사용해요!

Positive (긍정)	Negative (부정)	Question (의문)
I would	I wouldn't	Would **you**?
~할 거야 (나라면), ~하겠다	~ 안 할 거야 (난)	① ~할 거야? (너라면) ② ~해줄래? (부탁)

이렇게 만듭니다!

문장의 핵심단어인 '동사'를 넣습니다!

Positive (긍정)	Negative (부정)	Question (의문)
나라면 갈 거야. I would go.	난 안 갈 거야 I wouldn't go.	너라면 갈 거야? Would you go?

<비교분석>

"Can vs Could vs Would"

Can you?	~해줄래요? (~할 수 있겠어?)
Could you?	~해줄래요?
Would you?	~해줄래요? (그럴 의향이 있어?)

<심화표현>

내가 너라면,	If I were you,
내가 너 입장이라면,	If I were in your shoes,
내가 너 상황이라면,	If I were in your situation/position,

긍정문 I would

☞ 오른쪽 힌트를 이용해서, 직접 문장을 만들어보세요!

훈련용 MP3

정답확인 : P 285

01	나라면 살 거야. 정말 좋은 가격인데. 🔊	정말 좋은 가격 such a good price
02	나라면 이걸로 할 거야. 🔊	이거로 하다, 사다, 선택하다 go with
03	나라면 알텐데⋯ 🔊	
04	나라면 알고 싶을 거야. 🔊	
05	난 거기 가고 싶을 거야. 🔊	
06	나라면 이걸로 쓸 거야. 이게 쓰기 더 쉬워. 🔊	더 쉬운 easier
07	나라도 그 애 믿을 거야. 너의 잘못이 아니야. 🔊	
08	내가 너라면, 그거 할 거야. If I were you 🔊	
09	내가 너라면, 그걸 선택할 거야. 🔊	
10	내가 네 입장이라면, 그거 무시해 버릴 거야. 🔊	

긍정문 I would

☞ 오른쪽 힌트를 이용해서, 직접 문장을 만들어보세요!

11	나라면 행복할 거야.	
12	나라도 궁금할 거야.	궁금한 curious
13	나라면 정말 걱정될 거야.	정말 걱정하는 worried sick
14	난 멋진 걸 사겠어.	멋진 것 something cool
15	난 편한 걸 입겠어.	(뭔가) 편한 것 something comfortable
16	나도 그게 싫을거야. 이해해.	
17	나라도 동의하지 않겠어.	동의하지 않다 disagree
18	나라도 배신감 들 거야.	배신감 들다 feel betrayed
19	나라도 실망할 거야.	실망한 disappointed
20	나라도 쪽팔릴 거야.	쪽팔린 embarrassed

21	난 정말 멋진 차를 사겠어. 🔊	
22	난 최선을 다해보겠어. 우리 할 수 있어. 🔊	
23	난 세계를 여행하겠어. 너무 좋을 거야. 🔊	
24	그 애를 봐주겠어. 🔊	봐주다 go easy on 사람
25	계속 노력하겠어. 🔊	계속하다 keep -ing
26	난 계속 가겠어. 절대 포기하지 않을 거야. 🔊	포기하다 quit
27	난 밝은면을 볼 거야. 최소한 노력해 볼 거야. 🔊	밝은면을 보다 look at the bright side, 최소한 at least
28	그거 재미있겠다. 🔊	
29	그럼 좋겠어요. 고마워요. 🔊	
30	그러면 충분할 거예요. 🔊	

부정문 I wouldn't

☞ 오른쪽 힌트를 이용해서, 직접 문장을 만들어보세요!

31	나라면 그거 안 해.	
32	나라면 거기 안 가.	
33	나라면 그런 말 안 해. 너무 무례해.	무례한 rude
34	너라면 오래 버티지 않을 거야.	오래 버티다, 오래가다 last long
35	넌 좋아하지 않을 거야.	
36	넌 안 하겠지.	
37	넌 아무에게도 말 안 하겠지. 알아.	
38	넌 나 없이는 아무데도 안 갈 거지. 맞지?	
39	난 하나도 바꾸지 않을 거야.	하나도 a thing
40	나라도 안 올 거야.	도 either

부정문 I wouldn't

☞ 오른쪽 힌트를 이용해서, 직접 문장을 만들어보세요!

41	내가 너라면, 난 포기하지 않을 거야. 🔊	포기하다 give up/quit
42	**난 그 애 더 이상 안 볼 거야.** 🔊	
43	내가 네 상황이라면, 내 자신을 탓하지 않을 거야. 넌 최선을 다했어. 🔊	탓하다 blame
44	**내가 네 입장이라면, 심각하게 받아들이지 않을 거야.** 🔊	심각하게 받아들이다 take it seriously
45	나라면 걱정하지 않을 거야. 그거 잘 될 거야. 🔊	잘 되다 work out (well)
46	**내가 너라면, 지금 멈추지 않을 거야. 너 지금까지 너무 잘했어!** 🔊	
47	난 그 애한테 돈 빌려주지 않을 거야. 🔊	
48	**난 서두르지 않겠어. 난 천천히 할 거야.** 🔊	천천히 하다 take one's time
49	내가 너였다면, 그 애한테 아무 것도 기대하지 않을 거야. 🔊	
50	**나라면 그 애한테 강요하지 않을 거야.** 🔊	강요하다 force

51	난 개인적으로 받아들이지 않을 거야. (=기분 나쁘게 생각 안 할거야.)	개인적으로 받아들이다 take it personally
52	난 여기 있지 않을 거야.	
53	나라면 내 자신을 괴롭히지 않을 거야.	자신을 괴롭히는, 자책하는 hard on oneself
54	그건 좋지 않을 거야.	
55	지금은 좋지 않을 거야. 지금은 좋은 때가 아닐 거야.	
56	그럼 쉽지 않겠다.	
57	나라도 하기 싫을 거야.	
58	내가 너라도, 가기 싫을 거야.	
59	내가 네 상황이었다면, 위험을 감수하지 않을 거야. 너무 위험해.	위험을 감수하다 risk, 위험한 risky
60	내가 할 수 있다면, 할텐데. 하지만, 못 해.	내가 할 수 있다면, If I could,

의문문 Would you?

☞ 오른쪽 힌트를 이용해서, 직접 문장을 만들어보세요!

61	너라면 하겠니? 🔊	
62	넌 뭘 하겠니? 🔊	
63	넌 어느 걸 선택하겠어? 🔊	
64	내게 뭘 조언하겠어? 🔊	조언하다 advise
65	너라면 가겠어? 🔊	
66	너라면 뭐라고 하겠니? 🔊	
67	너가 내 입장이면, 이걸 어떻게 처리하겠니? 🔊	처리하다 take care of/handle
68	너가 나라면, 조용히 있겠어? 🔊	
69	너라면 다르게 하겠어? 🔊	다르게 differently
70	넌 어떻게 할 거야? 🔊	

의문문 Would you?

☞ 오른쪽 힌트를 이용해서, 직접 문장을 만들어보세요!

71	너라면 여전히 여기 있겠어?	
72	넌 어떻게 그걸 피하겠어? 방법을 알고 싶어.	방법 the way
73	넌 어떻게 그걸 해결하겠어? 네 조언이 필요해.	조언 advice
74	넌 어딜 가겠어?	
75	넌 어느 길을 선택하겠어?	어느 길 which way/ which path
76	여전히 날 사랑하겠어?	
77	뭘 추천할 거야?	
78	어떻게 '아니'라고 말하겠어? 거절하기 힘들어.	거절하다 refuse
79	그 애한테 어떻게 말할 거야?	
80	너라면 그게 좋을까?	좋아하다 like

81	넌 그 앨 어떻게 설득할 거야?	설득하다 persuade
82	날 어떻게 확신 시킬 거야?	확신 시키다 convince
83	너라면 뭘 살 거야?	
84	넌 뭘 바꾸겠어? 그리고 어떻게 바꿀 거야?	
85	너가 나였다면, 뭘 할 거야?	
86	너가 내 상황이었다면, 거절 하겠어?	
87	너가 나라면, 기분이 좋겠어?	
88	너라면 기분이 어떻겠어?	
89	그렇게 되게 만들기 위해 넌 뭘 하겠어? 난 뭘 하는 게 좋을까?	되게 만들다, 되게 하다 make-work
90	무슨 일이 있더라도 넌 항상 내 편 일거야?	무슨 일이 있더라도 no matter what

의문문 Would you?

☞ 오른쪽 힌트를 이용해서, 직접 문장을 만들어보세요!

91	그거 해줄래요? (그래줄래?) 🔊	
92	나랑 같이 가줄래? 🔊	
93	공항에서 나 픽업해줄래? 🔊	공항에서 from the airport
94	집에 오는 길에 그거 사다줄래요? 🔊	집에 오는 길 on the way home
95	그거 그만해줄래요? 🔊	그만하다 stop
96	그만 물어봐줄래요? 🔊	stop-ing
97	이거 나랑 바꿔줄래? 🔊	바꾸다 switch
98	나 좀 봐줄래요? 🔊	봐주다 go easy on 사람
99	좀 참아줄래? (인내심을 가져줄래?) 🔊	참는, 인내심을 가진, 조급하지 않은 patient
100	조용히 해줄래요? 🔊	

복습강의 MP3

Positive (긍정)		Negative (부정)		Question (의문)	
I am -ing	해, 하고있어 (지금)	I'm not -ing	안 해, 안하고있어	Are you -ing?	해? (지금) 하고 있어?
I 동사	해 (원래)	I don't	안 해	Do you?	해? (원래)
I will	할 걸, 할 거야 (예측)	I won't	안 할 걸, 안 할 거야	Will you?	할까? 할꺼야? (예측)
I think I'll	할 것 같아	I don't think I'll	안 할 것 같아	Do you think you'll	할 것 같아?
I may I might	할지도 몰라, 할 수도 있어	I may not I might not	안할지도 몰라, 안할 수도 있어	May I?	해도 돼요? (허락)
I 과거	했어, 했었어	I didn't	안 했어	Did you?	했어?
I was -ing	하고 있었어 (그때)	I wasn't -ing	안 하고 있었어	Were you -ing?	하고 있었어? (그때)
I have p.p.	① 해봤어 (경험) ②했어 (쭉, 지금까지)	I haven't p.p.	①안 해봤어 ②안 했어 (계속)	Have you p.p.?	①해봤어? ②했어? (계속)
I could	할 수 있었어 (능력)	I couldn't	못 했어	Could you? Could I?	해줄래요? 해도 돼요?
I would	할 거야 (나라면)	I wouldn't	안 할 거야	Would you?	할 거야?

01	너가 그거하면, 나도 할게.	23	너 올 때까지 아무것도 안 할게.
02	난 정말 이게 하고 싶어. [정말 so much]	24	너 그거 아직 하면 안 돼.
03	나 집에 가자마자, 이거 해야 돼.	25	난 그거 안 해. 난 그거 안 좋아해.
04	우리 이거 같이 하는 게 좋을 것 같아.	26	나 그거 안 해본지 오래됐다.
05	난 그거 나중에 할 것 같아. 지금은 그거 할 시간이 없어.	27	나 지금 아무것도 안 하는데. 만날래?
06	나 그건 나중에 할거야.	28	나라면 그거 안 해.
07	너 그거 여기서 해도 돼. 괜찮아.	29	나 그거 안 했어. 내가 아니야!
08	나 지금 뭔가하고 있는데. 이거 한 후에, 그거 할게.	30	나 그거 아직 안 했어.
09	나도 이번엔 그거 할지도 몰라.	31	나 아무것도 안 하고 있었어.
10	우리 지금 이거 하지 뭐.	32	이거 해줄래요?
11	나 그거 항상 해. [항상 all the time]	33	내일 뭐 할래?
12	나 그거 지난주에 했어.	34	나 이거 해야 돼? 왜 해야 돼?
13	나 이거 많이 해봤어.	35	넌 이번 주말에 뭐 할것 같아?
14	너가 전화했을 때, 내가 뭔가 하고 있었어. 왜 전화했었어?	36	저 이거 해도 되나요?
15	내가 너라면, 이거 할거야.	37	우리 뭐 할까?
16	난 그거 못 하겠어.	38	너가 내 입장이면, 뭘 할거야?
17	난 이번엔 그거 안 할 것 같아.	39	너 지금 뭐해? 만날 수 있어?
18	난 그거 안 할지도 몰라.	40	뭐 하고 있었어? 내가 방해했니?
19	난 그거 안 할거야. 이번엔 안 하기로 했어.	41	어제 뭐 했어?
20	너 그거 안 해도 돼.	42	이거 전에 해봤어?
21	나 그거 못 했어. 미안.	43	넌 내일 뭐 할거야?
22	난 이거 하고 싶지 않아.	44	우리 이거 어떻게 하는 게 좋을 것 같아?

정답확인 : P 288

일상

A: You look tired. Are you ok?

B: I am ok. I haven't slept well for a few days. I couldn't sleep at all last night.

A: I would be tired, too. Is something wrong?

B: No. Nothing is wrong. It is just., I (have) decided to quit my job.

A: Why did you decide to do that? When is your last day?

B: Tomorrow is my last day. I have a lot (of things) to do at work. And I am thinking about a new job.

A: I would be stressed out as well. Are you looking for a new job?

B: Yes, I am looking for a new job. But I don't know what to do.

A: When you finish work tomorrow, I think you should take a rest for a few days. You can think about it later.

B: I will be unemployed from tomorrow. It is a bit scary. I have never been unemployed before. / I haven't been unemployed before.

A: It would be scary. But it will/would be a new beginning.

B: Since I graduated(=left school), I have worked there. It has already been 10 years. It is hard to get a job these days.

A: If I were in your shoes, I wouldn't think about anything. You deserve some rest. / You deserve to rest.

B: Do you really think so?

A: Yes, I think so. When you feel better, you will know what to do. You always do.

B: Thank you. You are such a good friend.

A: Since we were children, we have been friends. I know you. You will be ok. Everything is going to work out well.

B: Thank you for saying that. I feel much better.

A: 너 피곤해보여. 괜찮니?

B: 괜찮아. 잠을 며칠 잘 못 잤어. 어젯밤엔 잠을 아예 못 잤어.

A: 나라도 피곤하겠다. 뭔가 잘못 됐니?

B: 아니. 아무것도 잘못 되지 않았어. 그냥. 내 일[my job] 그만두기로 했어.

A: 왜 그렇게 하기로 했어? 언제가 마지막 날이야?

B: 내일이 내 마지막 날이야. 회사에서 할 일이 너무 많아. 그리고, 새 직업에 대해서도 생각 중이고.

A: 나라도 스트레스 받겠어. [stressed out] 새 직업 찾고 있어?

B: 어, 새 직업 찾고 있어. 하지만, 뭘 할지 모르겠어.

A: 내일 일 끝나면, 며칠 쉬는 게 좋을 것 같아. 나중에 생각해 봐도 돼.

B: 내일부터는 나 백수일 거야. [백수 unemployed] 좀 겁나. [겁나는, 무서운 scary] 백수여본 적이 없어.

A: 겁나겠지. 하지만, 새로운 시작일 거야.

B: 학교 졸업한 후로, 나 거기서 일했어. 벌써 10년 됐어. 요즘 직장구하기 힘들잖아.

A: 내가 네 입장이라면, 난 아무것도 생각하지 않을 거야. 너 좀 쉬어도 돼. [해도 돼, 자격있어 deserve]

B: 진짜 그렇게 생각해?

A: 어, 그렇게 생각해. 기분 나아지면, 뭘 할지 너가 알거야. 너 항상 그렇잖아.

B: 고마워. 넌 정말 좋은 친구야. [정말 좋은 친구 such a good friend]

A: 우린 어렸을 때부터 친구잖아. 난 널 알아. 넌 괜찮을 거야. 모든 게 잘 될 거야.

B: 그렇게 말해줘서 고마워. 기분 훨씬 낫다.

일상

A: I want to lose (some) weight. If you were me, what would you do?

B: You don't have to lose weight. You look good. If I were in your shoes, I wouldn't want to lose weight.

A: I want to look better. I want to be healthy, too. What would you recommend?

B: How about yoga? Yoga is really good. But, if you do yoga, it takes time to lose weight.

A: I'd like to do something fun.

B: What about crossfit? You will/would like that. It is fun as well.

A: Do you think I'll lose weight fast if I do crossfit?

B: I think you will.

A: Which gym would you go (to)?

B: I would go to the gym close to(=near) my place.

A: I love beer. I drink a can of beer a day. Would you stop drinking beer ?

B: I don't like beer, so I wouldn't drink. A can of beer a day isn't bad.

A: Do you work out in the morning or in the evening?

B: I work out in the morning. But I think you should work out after you finish work in the evening.

A: 나 살을 좀 빼고 싶어. 네가 나라면 뭘 하겠어?

B: 살 안 빼도 돼. 너 좋아 보여. 내가 네 입장이라면, 살 안 빼고 싶을 것 같은데.

A: 난 더 좋아 보이고 싶어. 건강하고 싶기도 하고. 내게 뭘 추천 하겠어?

B: 요가는 어때? 요가 정말 좋아. 하지만, 요가하면, 살 빼는데 시간이 걸리지.

A: 난 재미있는 것 하고 싶어.

B: 크로스핏은 어때? 네가 좋아할거야. 재미있고.

A: 크로스핏하면 내가 살 빨리 뺄수 있을 것 같아?

B: 그럴 것 같아.

A: 너라면 어느 체육관으로 다닐거니?

B: 나라면 우리 집이랑 가까운 체육관으로 갈거야.

A: 난 맥주 너무 좋아해. 하루에 맥주 한 캔 마시는데. 너라면 맥주 마시는거 끊을 거야?

B: 난 맥주 안 좋아하니까. 나라면 안 마시겠지만. 하루에 맥주 한 캔 나쁘진 않지.

A: 넌 운동 아침에 하니 아님 저녁에 하니?

B: 난 아침에 하는데. 넌 퇴근하고 나서 저녁에 운동하는 게 좋을 것 같다.

정/답/체/크

Unit 1

1.   We are studying English now.
2.   I am working now. Can I call (you back) later?
3.   He is studying/working (very) hard now.
4.   We are going home now.
5.   Sally is coming now.
6.   I am making something now.
7.   We are driving/going to the airport now.
8.   We are waiting for you now.
9.   Shush! He/She is sleeping now.
10.   I am taking/having a shower now. I will be/go/come out soon.
11.   You are working late.
12.   I am getting a (little) bit hungry. How/What about you?
13.   I am eating/having lunch now. Do you want to/Would you like to join me?
14.   We are going out now. I have to hang up.
15.   He/She is lying.
16.   He/She is having fun/a good time now.
17.   (I'm) Sorry, I am driving now. I will call you (back) later.
18.   I am playing a game on my phone now. It is fun.
19.   We are doing something now. Can I do it later?
20.   I am joking/kidding.
21.   Somebody/Someone is sitting here. You can't take it.
22.   I am looking for my (cell/mobile)phone now.
23.   I am looking for something like this. Where is it?
24.   I am looking at (some) photos/pictures. I will show you a good one.
25.   The/My/Your phone is ringing.
26.   Hang on/Hold on. I am thinking about something.
27.   I am listening to it. Can you (just) leave it on?
28.   I am trying (hard/my best). I am going to finish it by today.
29.   You are looking good today!
30.   We are trying everything. We are doing/trying our best.
31.   It is raining.
32.   It is snowing outside. It is so/very/really beautiful.
33.   It is getting better.
34.   It is getting cold. Are you warm (enough)?
35.   It is getting worse.
36.   It is getting dark. I think we should go now.
37.   It is getting late. I will go out/leave now.
38.   It is getting bigger. What shall/should I do?
39.   It is getting harder.

40. It is working.
41. I am not watching it now. You can turn it off.
42. We are not going anywhere now.
43. I am not doing anything now. Do you want to(=Would you like to) meet?
44. I am not using it now. You can use it.
45. Nobody/No one is sitting here. You can take it.
46. I am not crying. My eyes are sore. / My eye is sore. / I have sore eyes.
47. This pen is not working.
48. I am not sleeping now.
49. I am not working now. I can talk.
50. I am not working today. It is my day off.
51. We are not waiting for anyone/anybody.
52. I am not doing it alone. My friends are helping (me).
53. I am not driving now.
54. We are not talking about you.
55. I am not planning anything.
56. I am not kidding/joking. I am serious.
57. It is not raining anymore. And it is not going to rain. You don't have to take an/the/ your umbrella.
58. It is not snowing now.
59. It is not working.
60. It is not getting better. We have to do something about that/it.
61. Are you doing something now? Are you busy?
62. What are you doing?
63. Where are you going? Can I come, too?
64. Are you going somewhere now? Are you in a hurry?
65. Are you listening to me?
66. Why are you laughing?
67. What are you looking at? What is it?
68. What are you looking for?
69. Are you looking for something? Is it this (one)?/Are you looking for this?
70. Who are you looking for?
71. Why are you looking at me like that? Stop it!
72. Are you eating something? What are you eating?
73. Are you cooking/making dinner now? What are you cooking?
74. What are you thinking about?
75. Are you waiting for someone/somebody?
76. Why are you crying? Are you ok? Are you sick?
77. What are you talking about/saying?
78. Are you using it now? (Or) can I borrow it?

79. Are you saving this seat?
80. Are you coming now? Where are you?
81. Are you kidding/joking?
82. What is he/she doing now? Is he/she working?
83. Are you watching it now? Or can I turn it off?
84. Who are you talking to? Are you talking to yourself?
85. What are you wearing?
86. Where are we going now?
87. Are you feeling better? How are you feeling?
88. What am I doing here?
89. What are you waiting for? Just go for it/Just do it!
90. What are you trying to do?
91. Is it raining again?
92. Is it snowing outside?
93. Is it working?
94. Is it getting better?
95. Is it getting bigger?
96. Is it getting easier?
97. Is it blinking? Is it on?
98. Why is it blinking? Is something wrong?
99. Why is it beeping? Can you have/take a look at it?
100. Why is it taking so/this long?

Review
1. I have to borrow it.
2. You can borrow it.
3. Do you want to(=Would you like to) borrow it? I am ok/fine.
4. I want to(=I'd like to) borrow it.
5. You can't borrow it.
6. I will borrow it. Thank you.
7. I should borrow it.
8. I can borrow it.
9. I don't want to(=I wouldn't like to) borrow it.
10. Shall we borrow it?
11. You don't have to borrow it. I can lend it to you.
12. We can't borrow it. We have to buy it.
13. Do I have to borrow it?
14. Can you borrow it?
15. I am not going to borrow it.

16. Which one do you want to(=would you like to) borrow? You can choose.
17. What do I have to borrow?
18. Should I borrow it?
19. Why do you want to(=would you like to) borrow it?
20. Which one shall I borrow?
21. Why do you have to borrow it?
22. Which one do you think I should borrow?
23. You shouldn't borrow it.
24. I am borrowing a book from my friend.
25. I am not borrowing money from him/her.
26. Why are you borrowing it from him/her?

Unit 2

1. We need it. Can we have it?
2. I need (some) help.
3. I understand. You don't have to explain (it to me).
4. He/She understands me.
5. I usually get up at 7 (o'clock).
6. He always gets up early.
7. I usually go to bed at 12 (o'clock).
8. He always goes to bed late.
9. I like/love animals.
10. Tom likes/loves this/it.
11. I prefer this (one). / I like this/it better.
12. Tom prefers coffee.
13. I hate this/it.
14. Jim hates it/this.
15. This store/shop opens at 9 and closes at 6.
16. I already know. / I know already.
17. Jim knows, too.
18. I have it/that.
19. He/She has a car.
20. We have time to do it/that.
21. I live in Seoul, and my mom lives in Gyeonggi-do.
22. I mean it/that.
23. I remember it/that.
24. He remembers everything.
25. I miss it/that.
26. He always does it/that.

27. I go there once a week.
28. He goes there every day.
29. We take/accept credit cards.
30. The/That store/shop sells socks, too. You can buy socks there.
31. It rains a lot here.
32. It hurts.
33. It works.
34. It breaks easily. You/We have to be careful.
35. It takes long.
36. It costs a lot (of money).
37. It takes an hour to come/get here.
38. It costs a lot (of money) to install that.
39. It looks good/great/nice.
40. It looks expensive.
41. I don't remember (it).
42. He doesn't know yet.
43. I don't understand him/her.
44. My friend doesn't eat kimchi. It is too spicy/hot for him.
45. You don't need it/this. You don't have to buy it.
46. I don't drink.
47. Jack doesn't smoke.
48. I don't like it/this.
49. He doesn't watch TV.
50. We don't go there often. /We don't often go there.
51. I don't have cash now.
52. I don't have time now.
53. I don't have time to go there.
54. We don't have time to do that/it.
55. He doesn't have time. He is busy.
56. I don't mean it/that. I am sorry.
57. It doesn't matter.
58. It doesn't work.
59. It doesn't take long.
60. It doesn't cost much (money).
61. Do you like it/this? What do you like?
62. Does Jenny like it/this?
63. Do you believe him/her? I can't believe him/her.
64. What does he/she want?
65. Where do you live?
66. Where do you work?

67. Where does Jack work?
68. What do you do (for a living)?
69. What does he do?
70. What time do you finish work?
71. Do you go there often? /Do you often go there?
72. What time do you close?
73. Do you see him/her often?/Do you often see him/her? How often do you see him/her?
74. Does Sam know, too?
75. What do you think?
76. Which one do you prefer/like better?
77. Do you need it/this? I want to/I'd like to give it to you.
78. Which one do I need?
79. Do you hate me? Why do you hate me?
80. Do you miss me?
81. What do you mean?
82. What does it/that mean?
83. Do you mean it? Are you serious?
84. So, what do you want from me?
85. How do I look? Do I look ok?
86. Do you have time?
87. Do you have time to come here?
88. Do you have time to talk to/with me?
89. Do I have time to go to the bathroom/toilet/restroom?
90. Do you have time to study? I don't have time to do anything.
91. Does it matter?
92. Does it work?
93. Does it hurt?
94. Does it break easily?
95. Does it happen often? /Does it often happen?
96. Does it fit?
97. Does it take long?
98. How long does it take?
99. How long does it take to go/get there?
100. How much does it cost?

Review

1. What shall we watch?
2. Do you want to(=Would you like to) watch it?
3. I have to watch it.
4. I don't want to(=I wouldn't like to) watch it.
5. What do you want to(=would you like to) watch?
6. You can watch it.
7. I will watch it later.
8. I don't have to watch it now.
9. You can't watch it. You are too young.
10. Should I watch it?
11. I want to(=I'd like to) watch it.
12. We should watch this movie this time.
13. I won't watch it.
14. I can't watch it. I don't like horror movies.
15. What should we watch?
16. Do I have to watch it?
17. I don't think you should watch it. It is scary.
18. Can you watch it with me?
19. Can I watch it, too?
20. Which one do you think we should watch?
21. I am watching it now. You can't change the channel(s).
22. What are you going to watch?
23. I don't watch TV often. / I don't often watch TV.
24. He watches TV every day.
25. What are you watching?
26. I am not watching it now. You can turn it off.
27. Do you watch TV? What do you usually watch?
28. I am going to watch that/the movie next week.

Unit 3

1. He/She will like/love it.
2. You have to meet Jennifer. You (two/guys) will get along.
3. You will have enough time. You don't have to worry.
4. You/We/I can ask her/him. He/She will help.
5. You will need it/this. You can take it.
6. They will get here/arrive soon.
7. Try it/this on. It will look good on you. /It'll suit you.
8. It will be easy.

9. It will be identical/the same.
10. He/She will be busy. We shouldn't bother him/her.
11. It will be cheap.
12. It will be ready by then.
13. It will rain later.
14. It will take long.
15. It will cost a lot (of money).
16. It will work. I am sure.
17. It will break down again.
18. Everything will be ok.
19. It will be a problem.
20. It will disappear soon.
21. He/She won't like it/that.
22. You won't need it/that.
23. It won't be easy.
24. It won't help. / It won't be helpful.
25. It won't snow.
26. It won't take long.
27. It won't cost much (money).
28. It won't hurt.
29. It won't work.
30. It won't happen again. I apologize.
31. Will you be (at) home at 5?
32. What time will you come/be back?
33. Will it rain?
34. Will it work? What do you think?
35. Will it take long? How long will it take? I don't have (much) time.
36. Will it change again? It often changes. / It changes often.
37. Will it look good on me? / Will it suit me? I hope so.
38. Will it happen again? I hope not.
39. Will you be ok? I am worried about you.
40. Will 5 (o'clock) be ok?
41. I think I'll be/stay (at) home tonight. You can call any time.
42. I think they'll get married soon.
43. I think Jim will help. He always says "yes".
44. I think everything will work out (well).
45. I think you will succeed. I believe in you!
46. I think it'll take about two hours.
47. I think it'll cost 20 dollars. Would you like to(=Do you want to) pay now?
48. I think it'll be expensive to fix (that).

49. I think it/this one will be better.
50. I think it'll get easier.
51. I don't think Paul will come.
52. I don't think I'll go.
53. I don't think I'll play tennis tomorrow. I am not (feeling) well.
54. I don't think you'll have a problem.
55. I don't think he/she'll have it/that.
56. I don't think it'll stop.
57. I don't think you'll regret (it). Just do it! / Just go for it!
58. I don't think he'll forget (about) it/that.
59. I don't think it'll get better.
60. I don't think it'll get worse.
61. When do you think you'll arrive/get here?
62. What do you think he/she will say?
63. What do you think I'll need?
64. What do you think you'll do?
65. Where do you think you'll go?
66. Do you think it'll fit?
67. How much do you think it'll weigh?
68. How long do you think you'll stay there?
69. Do you think we'll have time to go shopping?
70. Do you think I'll give up? I don't think so.
71. Do you think I'll do (it) well? Why do you think so?
72. How long do you think it'll take?
73. How much do you think it'll cost? Roughly?
74. Do you think it'll be possible?
75. Do you think it'll be a problem?
76. When do you think it'll be?
77. When do you think it'll be ready?
78. Do you think it'll be a good idea?
79. How much do you think it'll be?
80. Do you think it'll be enough?
81. When/If I see Jenny, I will tell her.
82. Until you come/get here, I will wait here.
83. When I go home, I will call you.
84. When/if he comes, I will let you know.
85. Before I go out, I will text you.
86. After I do/finish it, I will clean it.
87. As soon as I go/get home, I will email you.
88. If you ask him/her, he/she will help.

89. As soon as he/she comes/gets here, I will tell him/her.
90. Before I finish work, I will take care of/handle it.
91. When I go home, I will go straight to bed.
92. When I come back, I will buy a present/gift. I promise.
93. Until you decide, I will wait.
94. If/When you need help, can you let me know? I'd like to(=I want to) help.
95. If you do it, you will regret it. I don't think you should do it.
96. Before I do it, I will check it again.
97. As soon as you arrive/get home, can you text me?
98. When/If you see him/her, can you tell him/her?
99. After you finish/do it, can you call me?
100. When you are ready, can you leave (me) a message?

Review.
1. I want to (=I'd like to) study English.
2. If you want, you can study there.
3. It is hard to study here. I can't focus/concentrate.
4. I think I should study English hard this year.
5. When I go home, I will(=I am going to) study English.
6. I can study with you tomorrow.
7. If you want that/the job, you have to study hard.
8. I study English an hour every day/each day/a day. / I study English every day for an hour.
9. I am studying now. Can I do it later?
10. He studies really/very hard.
11. It is fun to study English.
12. I think it will be fun to study together.
13. I don't want to(=I wouldn't like to) study now. I will do it later.
14. I am not studying now. It is ok. We can talk now.
15. I can't study here. It is too/so/very/really loud.
16. I am not going to study with him/her. I am going to do it alone.
17. He doesn't study hard. He is not interested in/into studying.
18. I don't study English on Sunday(s).
19. If you don't want, you don't have to study.
20. Will I have time to study tomorrow? I don't think I will (have time).
21. What do you want to(=would you like to) study?
22. What are you going to study?
23. Do I have to study English?
24. Shall we study together? It will be fun. /It is going to be fun.

25. Do you study English every day? When do you study?
26. Do you have time to study?
27. I am into(=interested in) this field. What do you think I should study?
28. Are you studying now? What are you studying?
29. Can I study there?
30. When you grow up, what do you think you'll study?

Unit 4

1. We may go shopping later.
2. You may get/receive it soon.
3. You may feel sick.
4. You may regret it.
5. I may finish work late today.
6. You may laugh. But I am serious.
7. We may be lucky. Who knows?
8. You may be right.
9. I may be wrong.
10. He/She may be sick.
11. I might go to Thailand next week. A friend of mine lives there.
12. We might be/come late tomorrow. You can start/begin without us.
13. Danny might like it/this.
14. We might need it/this later. I am just going to keep it.
15. We might go to the (swimming) pool this weekend. Do you want to/ Would you like to come, too?
16. Tim might come, too.
17. Simon might come early. He always comes early.
18. You might lose it. It is better to leave it at home.
19. I might forget (about) it/that. Can you remind me later?
20. I can't leave/go out now. I am waiting for an important (phone) call. He might call soon.
21. It may rain this afternoon.
22. It may snow a lot tomorrow.
23. It may begin/start soon.
24. It may finish/end soon.
25. It may take long.
26. It may cost a lot (of money).
27. It may come this evening.
28. Your plan may work. I think you should try (it).
29. It may change again.

30. It may break down again.
31. It might be dangerous.
32. It might be too/very/so strong.
33. It might be empty.
34. It might be fake.
35. It might be weird/strange.
36. It might be my fault.
37. Something might be wrong.
38. It might be expensive.
39. It might be possible.
40. It might be awkward.
41. I may not go there. To be honest/frank, (=Honestly/Frankly) I don't want to(=wouldn't like to) go.
42. We may not stay/be there long.
43. He/She may not bring it.
44. We may not move.
45. He/She may not like it/that.
46. He/She may not agree.
47. They may not deliver.
48. They may not open on Sundays.
49. Jim may not want to go.
50. He/She may not want to see you.
51. It might not be a big deal. Until we know for sure, we shouldn't worry.
52. It might not be there.
53. It might not be ready yet.
54. It might not be enough.
55. It might not be a mistake. It might be on purpose.
56. It might not be serious.
57. It might not end/finish soon. It usually takes long.
58. It might not rain.
59. It might not work.
60. It might not take long.
61. May I go/leave now?
62. May I come/go in?
63. May I leave/go early today?
64. May I sit here?
65. May I ask something?
66. May I ask a question?
67. May I ask a personal question?
68. May I use it/this?

69. May I go to the bathroom/toilet?
70. May I use the bathroom/toilet?
71. May I try it/this?
72. May I go first?
73. May I see/look at it? / May I have/take a look (at it)?
74. May I ask why (that/it is)?
75. May I take this chair?
76. I am sorry to bother you. May I borrow this?
77. I am sorry to interrupt. May I go out/step out for a minute?
78. May I take this call/answer it?
79. May I try (it) again?
80. May I think about it? When I decide, I will let you know.
81. I might as well do it today.
82. I might as well go now.
83. I might as well buy it/this, too.
84. We might as well wait a bit longer.
85. It is raining outside. I might as well stay here.
86. I might as well (do it).
87. I might as well replace it/that, too.
88. I might as well gift wrap it/this.
89. I might as well talk/speak to the wall.
90. We might as well go somewhere else.
91. If I can't avoid it/that, I might as well enjoy it.
92. We might as well finish it now.
93. It is not far. I might as well walk there.
94. We might as well come clean/tell the truth. He/She will know.
95. We might as well stop here for a minute/while.
96. If I can't cancel it now, I might as well go.
97. I might as well tell you. Everybody/Everyone already knows. / Everybody knows already.
98. I might as well take (them) both(=both of them). We might need (them) both (=both of them).
99. We might as well go out/leave now.
100. If we can't get out of this situation, we might as well make the most of it.

Review.

1. If you want, I can stay here.
2. We have to stay here today.
3. Until you come, I will stay here.
4. I'd like to(=I want to) stay here for 3 nights.
5. When I go there, I am going to stay at my friend's place/house. My friend lives there.
6. You can stay here.
7. I might/may stay with my friend. I am not sure yet.
8. I think I'll stay (at) home all day. You can come any time.
9. I am staying at a hotel.
10. When he comes to(=he is in) Korea, He always stays with us.
11. We might as well stay here.
12. You should stay at my place/house.
13. I don't want to(=wouldn't like to) stay here.
14. I can't stay here any longer/anymore.
15. We don't have to stay here. We can go somewhere else.
16. I don't think I'll stay there.
17. He/She won't stay long.
18. We can't stay there long.
19. I am not staying there now. I am staying at my uncle's (place/house).
20. I don't stay there long. It is a (little) bit uncomfortable.
21. He may/might not stay with us. He prefers hotels.
22. Where are you going to stay?
23. How long do we have to stay there?
24. Where do you think we should stay?
25. Is it possible to stay here (for) one more night?
26. Can/May I stay here for a minute? I am so/very/really tired.
27. Do you want to(=Would you like to) stay at my place/house? If you want, you can (do that).
28. When you go to Japan, where do you stay? Is your family there? / Do you have your family there?
29. Where are you staying?
30. How long can you/I stay there?
31. Can you stay here for a minute/second/moment? I will be/come back soon.
32. Where do you think you'll stay? When you decide, can you let me know?

Unit 5

1. I came/got here 10 minutes ago.
2. I did it/that.

3. I bought it/this yesterday.
4. I slept well last night.
5. I cut my finger this morning.
6. I burned/burnt my hand yesterday.
7. I got up late this morning.
8. I made this for you.
9. I met Sam a few days ago/the other day.
10. We had/ate lunch together.
11. I found it.
12. I already knew (it). / I knew (it) already.
13. I went there with a/my friend.
14. I lost my/the ring. I am so/very/really upset.
15. He left/went out at 5 (o' clock).
16. I left my wallet/purse at home.
17. You did (it) well! I am proud of you!
18. I forgot (about it/that). I'm sorry.
19. I forgot to call you.
20. I forgot to tell you.
21. I brought the/my receipt.
22. He took it.
23. You already said that. / You said that already. (You already told me that. / You told me that already.) So, I know.
24. He told me. So, I knew.
25. I had a good/great/nice time. Thank you.
26. It hurt.
27. It took long/ a long time.
28. It took long(=a long time) to go/get there.
29. It cost a lot (of money).
30. It cost a lot (of money) to install (that).
31. I worked all day yesterday.
32. I watched TV.
33. You got here/arrived early.
34. We stayed there for a week.
35. It just began/started.
36. It finished/ended an hour ago.
37. It worked.
38. It rained all day yesterday.
39. It suddenly stopped. / It stopped suddenly. /Suddenly, it stopped.
40. It looked different.
41. I wanted to ask you something.

42. I wanted to go there.
43. I wanted to buy it/that.
44. I wanted to have it/that. Thank you.
45. I decided (it).
46. We decided to go there together.
47. I decided to do that/it.
48. I decided not to change anything.
49. I decided not to give up/quit.
50. I decided not to do it/that.
51. I didn't say anything.
52. I didn't tell anyone/anybody.
53. They didn't come.
54. I didn't do it/that.
55. I didn't buy anything. I didn't have my credit card.
56. I didn't have time.
57. I didn't have time to do anything.
58. I didn't have time to go there.
59. I didn't have time to call (you).
60. I didn't put it there. It is strange/weird.
61. I saw Jim yesterday, but/and he didn't say hello.
62. I didn't think about it/that.
63. I didn't know (it/that).
64. I didn't do anything.
65. I didn't mean it/that. I am sorry.
66. It didn't rain yesterday.
67. It didn't take long/ a long time.
68. It didn't break.
69. I didn't want to say anything. So I didn't (do/say that/it).
70. I didn't want to go anywhere. So I didn't go.
71. What did you do yesterday?
72. What did you say? I didn't hear it/you/that.
73. Why did you call (me)?
74. Why did you do that/it?
75. What did you see?
76. Where did you go?
77. How much did you pay (for it)?
78. Did you meet Simon yesterday? Where did you go?
79. Did you have a good/nice/great time?
80. Did you have a good/nice weekend?
81. When did you get here/come?

82. Did you wait long/(for) a long time? I am sorry (that) I am late.
83. Did you sleep well?
84. Did you eat/have lunch? What did you eat/have (for lunch)?
85. When did you get/come back?
86. How long did you stay there?
87. What did you buy/get?
88. Where did you buy/get it?
89. Did you bring the receipt?
90. Where did you get it?
91. Did you lose something? Are you looking for something?
92. Where did you put/leave it?
93. Did you hear the news?
94. How did you do that? / How did it happen?
95. Why did you hesitate?
96. Did you get it/understand?
97. Did it rain?
98. Did it take long/a long time? How long did it take?
99. Why did it take so/this long?
100. How much did it cost?

Review

1. If you are ok/fine (with it), I want to(=I'd like to) wait here.
2. Until I come, you have to wait here.
3. I can wait. It is ok.
4. I am going to wait (for) 10 more minutes.
5. I think we should wait.
6. You can wait here.
7. I will wait here for you. / I will wait for you here.
8. I am waiting for a/my friend. Can I order later?
9. We might as well wait here.
10. He is always late. And I always wait for him.
11. He may/might be waiting.
12. I waited for you.
13. It is not easy to wait. I don't like it.
14. I can't wait anymore/any longer. I am going to go.
15. You don't have to wait long/(for) a long time.
16. I don't want to(=I wouldn't like to) wait. I want to(=I'd like to) start/begin now.
17. I don't think it'll wait for us.
18. I am not waiting for anyone/anybody. I am alone here. / I am here alone.

19. He doesn't wait for anyone/anybody.
20. I didn't wait long/(for) a long time. I just got/came here.
21. Can you wait here for a minute/second/moment?
22. How long do I have to wait? Will it take long/ a long time?
23. Can we/I wait here?
24. Do you think we should wait?
25. Where are you going to wait?
26. Do you think he'll wait for us?
27. What are you waiting for? Just go for it/do it!
28. Where shall we wait?
29. Are you waiting for someone/somebody? Or do you want to(=would you like to) order now?
30. Did you wait long/(for) a long time? How long did you wait?
31. When you arrive/get there, can you wait for me? I think I'll get there/arrive in 5 minutes.
32. How long do you usually wait for it/that? Does it take long/a long time?

Unit 6

1. I was (at) home all day.
2. I was in bed.
3. I was exhausted (=very/so/really tired) last night.
4. I was starving (=so/very/really hungry).
5. I was in Hong Kong this time last year. It was so/very/really good.
6. Sorry, I was busy working.
7. Sorry, I was in a hurry.
8. I was (talking) on the phone.
9. I was on the way to work.
10. I was sick a few days ago/the other day.
11. I was there (,too) yesterday.
12. I was a (little) bit annoyed because of him/her. / Because of him/her, I was a (little) bit annoyed.
13. He was (all) alone.
14. They were late, so I was angry/mad. / I was angry because they were late.
15. I was so/very/really sleepy. So I fell asleep.
16. I was so/very/really excited.
17. You were lucky.
18. I was on your side. I am always on your side.
19. I was very/so/really surprised/shocked.
20. He was very/so/really nervous.

21. It was expensive.
22. It was very easy.
23. It was identical/the same.
24. It was weird/strange.
25. It was boring.
26. It was wet.
27. It was slippery.
28. It was very/so/really far.
29. It was delicious/yum/yummy.
30. It was here 5 minutes ago. It is weird/strange.
31. I wasn't hungry. So I didn't eat much.
32. I wasn't close to him/her.
33. Unfortunately, he wasn't lucky.
34. I wasn't annoyed.
35. I wasn't worried about anything.
36. I wasn't afraid/scared of anything.
37. I wasn't frustrated.
38. I wasn't happy.
39. I wasn't satisfied.
40. I wasn't sad. I was ok/fine.
41. It wasn't (very) good.
42. It wasn't comfortable.
43. It wasn't hard. But, it wasn't easy either.
44. The weather wasn't good/nice yesterday.
45. It wasn't serious.
46. It wasn't hard/difficult.
47. It wasn't there.
48. It wasn't my style/cup of tea.
49. It wasn't your fault.
50. It wasn't a good experience. That/It is all.
51. Why were you late?
52. Why were you angry/mad yesterday?
53. Where were you? I didn't see you.
54. Were you busy? / Were you in a hurry?
55. How old were you?
56. Was it a good choice?
57. Was it a misunderstanding?
58. Was it crowded?
59. Was it your decision?
60. Was it your intention? What was your intention?

61. How was the movie? Was it good?
62. How was the weather? Was the weather good/nice?
63. I like your jacket. / Your jacket is nice/cool. Was it expensive?
64. How much was it?
65. How was your day? Was it a good day?
66. How was your weekend?
67. Was it far? How long did it take?
68. When was your birthday?
69. Was it ok?
70. Was it fun? / Was it funny?
71. When I was little/a child/a kid/a student/young, I was shy.
72. When I was there, you were there, too.
73. When you were sick, I was worried about you.
74. When I was 20 (years old), I was bold.
75. When we were students, we were so/very/really naïve.
76. When my brother/sister was 10 (years old), he/she was so/very/really cute.
77. When he/she was little/a kid/a child, he/she was selfish.
78. When I was a high school student, it was famous.
79. When we were babies, we were always happy.
80. When we were there, everyone/everybody was there.
81. When I called you, you were busy.
82. When you came, I was happy/glad to see you.
83. When you told him/her, was he/she alone?
84. When I asked him/her, he/she was kind/friendly.
85. When I heard that, I was shocked.
86. When we found it/this, we were relieved.
87. When I won, I was so/very/really happy.
88. When you lost it/that, you were depressed/blue.
89. When you ignored me, I was angry/mad.
90. When you gave it to me, I was surprised.
91. When I was little/a child/a kid, I was afraid/scared of dogs.
92. When I went there, it was my first time.
93. When I came/got home, I was exhausted (=very/so/really tired).
94. When I remembered it/that, it was so/very/too/really late.
95. When I called, you were not there. Where were you?
96. When we got there/arrived, nobody/no one was there.
97. When he came, I was out.
98. When I bought/got it, it was 80 dollars.
99. When you saw him, how was he?
100. When it happened, I was shocked/very surprised.

Review

1. I have to make something now. I don't have time now.
2. I want to(=I'd like to) make something for him/her.
3. I am going to make a birthday card.
4. It is easy to make.
5. I can make it. It is easy.
6. You can make anything.
7. I should make a small one this time.
8. After I finish/do it/this, I will make it/that.
9. I am making something now.
10. I make it well. I am good at making something.
11. I may/might make a birthday cake this year. I am learning how to make a cake.
12. We might as well make it/this together.
13. I made it/this for you. Do you like it?
14. We may/might not make anything this year.
15. It is not hard/difficult to make. Anyone/anybody can do it.
16. I don't want to (=I wouldn't like to) make it/that. I just want to (=I'd would like to) buy it.
17. I am not going to make anything. I am going to order everything.
18. I am not making anything. I already finished it/I finished it already.
19. I didn't make it/this. I bought it.
20. I can't make it/that. I am not good at it.
21. Can you make it like this?
22. Why do I have to make it?
23. When you made it, was it easy?
24. How do you make it/this?
25. How did you make it/this?
26. Where can you/I make it/this?
27. What are you going to make? Can we do it together?
28. What do you want to(=would you like to) make?
29. Shall we make it together?
30. What should we make?
31. What are you making?
32. Did you make it/this?

Unit 7

1. I was thinking about you.
2. Sorry, I was thinking about something else.
3. I was just leaving.
4. I was going home.

5. I was doing something.
6. I was reading a book.
7. I was waiting for you.
8. Thank you. I was looking for it/this. Where did you find it?
9. I was working out/exercising.
10. I was texting you.
11. We were sleeping.
12. I was driving then.
13. I was using it/this.
14. I was cooking. Stay for dinner.
15. We were just talking about you.
16. Everybody/everyone was rooting for you.
17. Everybody/everyone was working hard.
18. Someone/somebody was snoring. It was so/very/really funny.
19. I was taking a selfie.
20. You were looking at something. What was it?
21. When I got there/arrived, Tim was waiting.
22. When you came, I was watching TV.
23. When he/she came in, we were talking about him/her.
24. When you rang the (door)bell, I was taking/having a shower.
25. When I saw him/her, he/she was working. He/she was busy.
26. When you called, I was thinking about you.
27. When I was waiting for you, I saw Jim.
28. When/while I was cooking, I cut my finger.
29. When/while I was washing/doing the dishes, I broke a glass.
30. When/while I was working out/exercising, I hurt myself.
31. It was raining cats and dogs.
32. It was snowing. Everything was white. It was so/very/really beautiful.
33. She was wearing a very beautiful dress. She looked hot/good/gorgeous.
34. He was wearing a black jacket.
35. Everyone/everybody was just standing there, (and they were) doing nothing.
36. Nobody/no one was using it/that, so I used it.
37. Nobody/no one was sitting here, so I brought it.
38. Nobody/no one was doing it/that, so I did it.
39. Nobody/no one was watching it/that, so I turned it off.
40. Nobody/no one was talking/speaking, so it was very/so/really quiet.
41. It is ok. I wasn't sleeping.
42. I wasn't doing anything.
43. I wasn't going anywhere.
44. I wasn't thinking about anything.

45. I wasn't crying.
46. I wasn't driving fast(=speeding). I was going/doing 50.
47. Sorry, I wasn't listening. What did you say?
48. Sorry, I wasn't watching it. / I wasn't looking at it.
49. I wasn't using it/this. You can take it/this.
50. We weren't talking about you.
51. When you called, I wasn't doing anything.
52. When you came, I wasn't working.
53. When I saw you earlier, I wasn't going to the store/shop.
54. I wasn't paying attention.
55. Turns out, I wasn't doing it properly.
56. I wasn't saying anything.
57. I wasn't feeling good.
58. I wasn't feeling well.
59. He wasn't telling the truth.
60. I wasn't faking (it). I was really sick.
61. Were you using it/this?
62. Were you listening to it/this?
63. Were you sleeping? Did I wake you up?
64. Were you watching it?
65. Were you working?
66. Were you waiting for someone/somebody?
67. Were you waiting for me? Did you wait long/(for) a long time?
68. Were you looking for something? Did you find it?
69. What were you looking for? If you tell me, I will help (you).
70. Were you going home? / Were you on the way home?
71. Where were you going?
72. What were you doing?
73. Were you doing something? Do you have time to talk/chat?
74. Were you talking about me?
75. What were you talking about?
76. Were you speeding/driving fast?
77. How fast were you driving/going?
78. What were you thinking about?
79. Why were you running?
80. Were you cooking something?
81. What were you doing there?
82. What was he/she doing?
83. What was I saying?
84. What was I doing?

85. What was I looking for?

86. Where were you sitting?

87. What were you trying to do?

88. What were you trying to say/tell me?

89. Who were you talking/speaking to?

90. Were you studying?

91. When I called, what were you doing?

92. When you saw him, what was he doing?

93. When you got/went there, was he/she waiting?

94. Were you singing?

95. What were you practicing?

96. How were you feeling?

97. Why were you(two/guys) fighting/arguing?

98. Why were you avoiding him/her?

99. What were you hiding?

100. Why were you whispering?

Review

1. I want to(=I'd like to) drive.

2. I will drive.

3. If you want, I can drive.

4. We have to drive there. It is very/too/so/really far.

5. I think we should drive down.

6. I am going to drive there.

7. If you are ok, you can drive.

8. I am driving now. As soon as I get there/arrive, I will call (you).

9. We may/might drive there.

10. When you called, I was driving.

11. He drives well. / He is a good driver.

12. We might as well drive there.

13. I think we will drive.

14. It is better to drive there.

15. We drove there. It took an hour.

16. I don't want to(=I wouldn't like to) drive. I'm exhausted (=very tired).

17. You can't drive like this.

18. We are not going to drive there. We are going to take a train.

19. I don't have to drive.

20. I can't drive.

21. I don't think we will drive there. We may/might take a bus.

22. I didn't drive. He did/drove.
23. I wasn't driving fast.
24. He doesn't drive. He doesn't have a driver's license.
25. Can you drive?
26. Can I drive?
27. Are you going to drive there?
28. Did you drive here? How long did it take?
29. When I called, were you driving?
30. Are you driving now?
31. Do you drive? Do you have a car?
32. Do you think you will drive? I think I will walk.

Unit 8

1. I have done it before.
2. I have met her/him before.
3. I have heard it/that.
4. I have seen her/him before, but I don't remember where (it was).
5. I have used it before.
6. We have tried it. Do you remember(it)?
7. I have thought about it. And I (have) decided to go there.
8. I have seen the/that movie 3 times.
9. We have met before. It was last year.
10. I have read it. It is a good/nice/great book.
11. I have been to the bank.
12. We have been there many times.
13. I have been here before.
14. I have been to the bathroom/toilet/restroom.
15. We have been here a few times before.
16. I have been to Jeju Island 3 times. I like/love Jeju island.
17. He/She has been to Japan many times. His/Her family is there. (= He/She has his/her family there.)
18. He/She has been to many countries. He/she travels a lot.
19. I have been here twice.
20. I have been to China once. I went there last year. I want to(=I'd like to) go there again.
21. I have lived here for 3 years.
22. I have worked here since 2017.
23. We have known each other long/ for a long time. We first met in 2002.
24. I have had it for about 6 months.
25. I have driven that/the car long/ for a long time. I want(=I'd like) a new car now.

26. Since I got up this morning, I have had a headache.
27. Since I was 20 (years old), I have wanted this moment.
28. He has been in Korea for 2 years. He came to Korea 2 years ago.
29. I have always wanted to have it/this. Since I turned 30 (years old).
30. I have always wanted to meet you. I have heard a lot about you. It is so/very/really nice to meet you.
31. We have been together for 3 years.
32. I have been busy recently.
33. I have been worried about you.
34. It has been good so far. / So far, so good.
35. I have been well/good. How/What about you?
36. It has been cold recently.
37. He/She has been a teacher for a long time.
38. Since we were kids/children/little, we have been best friends.
39. He/She has been in the/a hospital for a week. I am going to visit (=go and see) him/her tomorrow.
40. You have been grumpy all morning. What's wrong? / What's the matter?
41. I haven't thought about it/that (before).
42. I haven't done/tried it/this. So I don't know how to use it.
43. I haven't used it yet.
44. I have seen her/him a few times before, but I haven't spoken/talked to her/him.
45. I haven't had time to do it/this.
46. I haven't seen the/that movie yet. Shall we watch it together?
47. He hasn't come yet.
48. It hasn't arrived yet. When did you send it?
49. Since you bought/got it for me, I haven't used anything else.
50. Since it happened, I haven't seen him/her.
51. I haven't been there yet.
52. I haven't been here before. It is my first time.
53. We haven't been to Jeju island yet.
54. I haven't been to Europe.
55. I haven't been to the post office yet. I haven't had time.
56. We haven't been there long/ for a long time. Do you want to (=Would you like to) go there today?
57. The weather hasn't been good recently.
58. Since then, it hasn't been the same. Everything feels different.
59. It hasn't been that long. It has been about 5 minutes.
60. You have never been on time. / You haven't been on time before. You are always late. What is your excuse (for) this time?
61. We haven't seen each other long/for a long time. It has been really/so/very long.

62. I haven't worked out/exercised for a few months.
63. I haven't played golf for a year.
64. I haven't worked here long/for a long time. I started/began last December.
65. I haven't done it long/for a long time.
66. I haven't eaten anything since breakfast.
67. I haven't been here long/for a long time. I arrived/got here 5 minutes ago.
68. I haven't spoken to him/her for a few months.
69. I haven't had any problems since then.
70. He/She hasn't left/gone out yet. He/She is still here.
71. Have we met before? You look familiar.
72. Have you read this book?
73. Have you thought about it? What is your decision?
74. Have you tried it a lot/many times? You do it so/very/really well. / You are doing it so well. / You are good at it.
75. How many times have you done it?
76. I am looking for my/the car key. Where has it gone? Have you seen it?
77. Have you tried it/this? It is so/very/really delicious/yum/yummy.
78. Have you used this/it before? Do you know how to use it?
79. How many times have I told you? You can't do it yet. It/Now is not the time.
80. How long have you been in Korea? You speak Korean well. / You speak good Korean.
81. Where have you been? I was looking for you. / I have been looking for you.
82. Have you been to the post office?
83. Have you been to this restaurant before?
84. Have you been to Australia?
85. Have you been here before? Is it your first time?
86. Have you been to Busan?
87. Long time no see. Have you been well? How have you been?
88. Have you been busy recently?
89. Have you been sick? How long have you been sick?
90. How has your day been?
91. How long have you worked here?
92. How long have you lived there?
93. How long has it been?
94. How long have you been here? When did you come/get here?
95. How long have you been married?
96. How long has it been like this?
97. How long have you known?
98. How long have you been a writer/an author?
99. How long have you known each other?

100. How long has he/she been your best friend?

Review

1. I can read it without (my/the) glasses.
2. I want to (=I'd like to) read it without (my/the) glasses.
3. You have to read it. It is a good book.
4. You can read it. You don't need my permission.
5. I think we should read this book this month.
6. After I read it first, I will let you know. / I will read it first, and (I will) let you know.
7. It is hard/difficult to read this book.
8. I am going to read a book.
9. I might as well read this book.
10. I am reading a book now.
11. He reads a lot. He likes/loves books.
12. I read it last month. It was good/nice/great/excellent.
13. I have read that/the book. It was fine/ok.
14. When you came, I was reading this book. It is pretty/quite interesting.
15. You can't read it. It is my diary.
16. I can't read it. My eyes are tired.
17. I don't want to(=I wouldn't like to) read anything.
18. You don't have to read it. I will read it (for you).
19. He may/might not read (a book/books). He doesn't like books.
20. I am not reading anything.
21. I haven't read it yet.
22. I won't read it without your permission.
23. I don't read (books). I don't have time to read.
24. I haven't read (books) long/for a long time.
25. I wasn't reading anything.
26. I didn't read your diary.
27. Can I/May I read it?
28. Can you read it?
29. Which book shall we read this month?
30. What do you want to (=would you like to) read?
31. Do you read (books)? I don't read (books).
32. Should we read it?
33. What are you reading?
34. When I came/got here, you were reading something. What were you reading?
35. Are you reading something? What are you reading?
36. Have you read this book?

Unit 9

1. When I was little/a child/a kid/a student/young, I could run really/very/so fast.
2. I could play the piano very well.
3. When I was in my 20's, I could do that, too.
4. I could drink all night a few years ago.
5. I could type really/so/very fast.
6. He could swim very well before the/that incident. He was very/so/really active.
7. He could play tennis all day before the/that accident.
8. When we were students, we could hang out every day.
9. Nobody/No one could stop him/her. He/She was stubborn.
10. Nothing could change my mind.
11. I couldn't do anything yesterday. I was exhausted (=so/very/really tired).
12. He couldn't come.
13. Sorry, I couldn't come yesterday. I didn't have time.
14. I am afraid I couldn't finish it. / I couldn't do it/them all.
15. I couldn't tell anyone/anybody.
16. I couldn't say anything.
17. I couldn't believe it.
18. I couldn't write anything here. What do I have to write (down) here?
19. I was exhausted(=very tired) last night. But I couldn't sleep at all.
20. I was very tired. So I couldn't get up early this morning.
21. I couldn't even hear the alarm.
22. I saw Jim yesterday, but I couldn't tell him.
23. I couldn't find your (phone) number. So I couldn't call (you).
24. I couldn't do (my) homework. I didn't have time.
25. He/She spoke/talked so/very/really fast, so I couldn't understand.
26. I couldn't eat anything. I didn't want to eat anything.
27. I couldn't take a picture/photo.
28. I couldn't speak English at all then.
29. I couldn't find anything. I was frustrated. / It was frustrating.
30. I couldn't move.
31. Sorry. I couldn't help you.
32. I couldn't choose. I liked/loved all/everything/all of them.
33. I couldn't buy/get it. I left my purse/wallet at home.
34. I couldn't recognize him/her. He/She looked so/very/really different.
35. I couldn't use it. I don't know how to use it.
36. I couldn't buy/get anything. I didn't know what to buy/get.
37. I couldn't decide. I don't know what to do.
38. I couldn't decide where to go.
39. I couldn't say a word. I didn't know what to say.

40. I couldn't stay/keep still.
41. I couldn't bring it. It was very/so/really/too heavy.
42. I couldn't understand him/her.
43. I couldn't stop crying.
44. It was so/very/really funny, (that) I couldn't stop laughing.
45. I was so/very/really happy. I couldn't stop smiling.
46. We couldn't win. We lost.
47. I couldn't sleep well. I am so/really/very tired. (=I am exhausted.)
48. I couldn't forgive him.
49. I couldn't focus/concentrate. It was so/very/really noisy/loud.
50. I couldn't persuade him/her. Never mind.
51. I couldn't lie.
52. I couldn't find (it) out.
53. I couldn't remember anything.
54. I couldn't memorize it. It is hard/difficult.
55. I was furious (=so/very/really angry/mad). I couldn't calm (myself) down.
56. I couldn't afford it/that. / I couldn't afford to buy it/that.
57. I couldn't fix/solve it/that. I am just going to let it go.
58. I couldn't enjoy myself. My mind was elsewhere/ somewhere else.
59. I couldn't love myself then.
60. I couldn't call you. Sorry.
61. Could you do this/it?
62. Could you do me a favor?
63. Could you call us back in 10 minutes?
64. Could you come (a little bit) earlier?
65. Could you say that again (=repeat that)?
66. Could you speak slowly?
67. Could you bring it/that?
68. Could you wait (for) a minute/moment/second?
69. Could you email me?
70. When you decide, could you let me know?
71. Could you wait for me?
72. Could you show me something else?
73. Could you move over a little/a bit?
74. Could you explain it to me?
75. Could you show me how to use it/this?
76. Could you teach me how to do it/this?
77. Could you help me with it/this?
78. Could you double check (=check it again) ?
79. Could you hold my hand(s)?

80. Could you hand me my phone?
81. Could I sit here?
82. Could I go now?
83. Could I ask something?
84. Could I ask a personal question?
85. Could I speak/talk to a/the manager?
86. Could I take it?
87. Could I decide later? As soon as I decide, I will call you.
88. Could we talk about something else?
89. Could we meet sometime next week?
90. Could we change the subject? I don't want to(=I wouldn't like to) talk about that/it.
91. Could I pick it up this evening?
92. Could I drop it off tomorrow?
93. Could I have time to think about it? I need more time.
94. Could I choose/pick this time? I want to(=I'd like to) choose/pick this time.
95. My phone is dead. Could I use your phone?
96. Could I see/look at your samples?
97. It is a (little) bit warm/hot in here. Could I leave it open?
98. Could I have (some/a glass of) water, please?
99. Could I have a plate/an extra plate, please?
100. I have a lot(of things) to do today. Could I take a rain check?

Review

1. I want to(=I'd like to) use this (one) instead of that.
2. You have to use it.
3. I should use it.
4. It is easier to use (this).
5. I will use it.
6. You can use mine.
7. I can use it. I know how to use it.
8. I am going to use it.
9. We might as well use it.
10. I have used it. It is easy to use.
11. I am using it now.
12. I usually use it.
13. I used it last night.
14. I was using it.
15. I have used it for 3 years.
16. I can't use it. Can you show me how to use it?

17. You can't use your phone here.
18. I am not using it. You can use it.
19. He may/might not use it. He bought/got a new one.
20. I haven't used it for a long time.
21. I haven't used it. Is it easy to use?
22. I didn't use it.
23. I don't use it. I have mine.
24. I wasn't using it. I was using mine.
25. I couldn't use it at all. It is useless.
26. Which one do you think you will use this time?
27. Which one do you think we should use?
28. Which one do I have to use here?
29. Can/Could you use this instead of that?
30. Were you using it?
31. Have you used it before?
32. Can/Could/May I use it?
33. Are you using it? Or can/could/may I take it?
34. Which one are you going to use?
35. How long have you used it?
36. Which/What brand do you use?

Unit 10
1. I would buy/get it. It is such a good price.
2. I would go with it/this.
3. I would know (it).
4. I would want to know.
5. I would want to go there.
6. I would use this/it. It is easier to use.
7. I would believe him/her, too. It is not your fault.
8. If I were you, I would do it/that.
9. If I were you, I would choose/pick it/that.
10. If I were in your shoes, I would ignore it/that.
11. I would be happy.
12. I would be curious, too/as well.
13. I would be worried sick.
14. I would buy something cool.
15. I would wear something comfortable.
16. I would hate it, too/as well. I understand.
17. I would disagree, too/as well.

18. I would feel betrayed, too/as well.
19. I would be disappointed, too/as well.
20. I would be embarrassed, too/as well.
21. I would buy a really cool/nice car.
22. I would do/try my best. We can do it.
23. I would travel the world. It would be so/really/very good.
24. I would go easy on him/her.
25. I would keep trying.
26. I would keep going. I would never give up/quit.
27. I would look at the bright side. I would try (hard) at least.
28. That/It would be fun.
29. That/It would be good/nice/great. Thank you.
30. That/It would be enough.
31. I wouldn't do it.
32. I wouldn't go there.
33. I wouldn't say that. It is so/very/really rude.
34. You wouldn't last long.
35. You wouldn't like it.
36. You wouldn't do it/that.
37. You wouldn't tell anybody/anyone. I know.
38. You wouldn't go anywhere without me. (Am I/Is that) Right?
39. I wouldn't change a thing.
40. I wouldn't come, either.
41. If I were you, I wouldn't give up/quit.
42. I wouldn't see him anymore.
43. If I were in your position/situation, I wouldn't blame myself. You did your best.
44. If I were in your shoes, I wouldn't take it seriously.
45. I wouldn't worry. It will work out (well). / It is going to work out (well).
46. If I were you, I wouldn't stop now. You have done so well so far.
47. I wouldn't lend (any) money to him. / I wouldn't lend him (any) money.
48. I wouldn't hurry/rush. I would take my time.
49. If I were you, I wouldn't expect anything from him.
50. I wouldn't force/push him.
51. I wouldn't take it personally.
52. I wouldn't be/stay here.
53. I wouldn't be hard on myself.
54. It/That wouldn't be good/nice.
55. Now wouldn't be good. Now wouldn't be a good time.
56. That/It wouldn't be easy (then).
57. I wouldn't want to do that, either.

58. (If I were you,) I wouldn't want to go, either.
59. If I were I your situation, I wouldn't risk (it). It is too risky.
60. If I could, I would (do that). But I can't (do that).
61. Would you do it?
62. What would you do?
63. Which one would you choose/pick?
64. What would you advise me?
65. Would you go?
66. What would you say?
67. If you were in my shoes, how would you take care of(=handle) it/this?
68. If you were me, would you be quiet?
69. Would you do it differently?
70. How would you do it?
71. Would you still be/stay here?
72. How would you avoid it/that? I want to(=I'd like to) know the way.
73. How would you solve/fix it/that? I need your advice.
74. Where would you go?
75. Which way/path would you choose/pick?
76. Would you still love me?
77. What would you recommend?
78. How would you say "NO"? It is hard/difficult to refuse.
79. How would you tell him/her?
80. Would you like it/that?
81. How would you persuade him/her?
82. How would you convince me?
83. What would you buy/get?
84. What would you change? And how would you change it/that?
85. If you were me, what would you do?
86. If you were in my shoes, would you refuse/say no?
87. If you were me, would you be happy?
88. How would you feel?
89. What would you do to make it work/happen? What should I do?
90. Would you be (always) on my side no matter what?
91. Would you do that/it?
92. Would you go/come with me?
93. Would you pick me up from the airport?
94. Would you buy/get it on the way home?
95. Would you stop that/it? Would you stop doing that/it?
96. Would you stop asking (me(that))?
97. Would you switch/change/trade it with me?

98. Would you go easy on me?
99. Would you be patient?
100. Would you be quiet?

Review

1. If you do it/that, I will do it, too.
2. I want to(=I'd like to) do it so much.
3. As soon as I go/get home, I have to do it.
4. I think we should do it together.
5. I think I will do it later. I don't have time to do it now.
6. I am going to do it later.
7. You can do it here. It is ok.
8. I am doing something. After I do it, I will do that.
9. I may/might do it this time.
10. We might as well do it now.
11. I do it all the time.
12. I did it last week.
13. I have done it many times/a lot (of times).
14. When you called, I was doing something. Why did you call (me)?
15. If I were you, I would do it.
16. I can't do it.
17. I don't think I will do it this time.
18. I may/might not do it.
19. I am not going to do it. I (have) decided not to do it this time.
20. You don't have to do it.
21. I couldn't do it. Sorry.
22. I don't want to (=I wouldn't like to) do it.
23. Until you get here/come, I won't do anything.
24. You can't do it yet.
25. I don't do it. I don't like it.
26. I haven't done/tried it long/for a long time.
27. I am not doing anything. Do you want to (=Would you like to) meet?
28. I wouldn't do it.
29. I didn't do it. It isn't me. / It wasn't me.
30. I haven't done it yet.
31. I wasn't doing anything.
32. Could/Can/Would you do it?
33. What do you want to(=would you like to) do tomorrow?
34. Do I have to do it? Why do I have to do it?

35. What do you think you will do this weekend?
36. Can/Could/May I do it?
37. What shall we do?
38. If you were in my shoes, what would you do?
39. What are you doing? Can you meet?
40. What were you doing? Did I interrupt?
41. What did you do yesterday?
42. Have you done it before?
43. What are you going to do tomorrow?
44. How do you think we should do it?

기초영어 1000문장 말하기 연습2

2020년 3월 16일 초판 1쇄 발행
2024년 7월 1일 초판 3쇄 발행

지 은 이 | 박미진
펴 낸 이 | 서장혁
기획편집 | 이경은
디 자 인 | 정인호

펴 낸 곳 | 토마토출판사
주　　소 | 서울특별시 마포구 양화로 161 케이스퀘어 727호
T E L | 1544-5383
홈페이지 | www.tomato4u.com
E-mail | support@tomato4u.com
등　　록 | 2012. 1. 11.
I S B N | 979-11-90278-21-8 (14740)